RISCH
3275 LUCIA AVE.
EUREKA, CA 95501

D0045908

TOUGH LOVE

Pauline Neff

TOUGH LOVE

How Parents Can Deal with Drug Abuse

Abingdon   Nashville

TOUGH LOVE: HOW PARENTS CAN DEAL WITH DRUG ABUSE

Copyright © 1982 by Pauline Neff

All rights reserved.
No part of this book may be reproduced in any manner
whatsoever without written permission of the publisher
except brief quotations embodied in critical articles or
reviews. For information address Abingdon,
Nashville, Tennessee

Library of Congress Cataloging in Publication Data

NEFF, PAULINE, 1928-
  Tough love.
  1. Drug abuse—Case studies. 2. Children—Drug
use—Case studies. 3. Parent and child 4. Palmer
Drug Abuse Program.   I. Title.
  RC564.N4   362.2'9386   81-17682   AACR2

ISBN 0-687-42406-2

MANUFACTURED BY THE PARTHENON PRESS AT
NASHVILLE, TENNESSEE, UNITED STATES OF AMERICA

To my family with love

Contents

TOUGH LOVE

Preface

When Father Charles Wyatt-Brown, rector of the Palmer Memorial Episcopal Church in Houston, gave ex-heroin addict Bob Meehan a job as custodian, he did not know he was founding a drug abuse program, too. At first Father Charlie simply encouraged Bob to tell the teen-agers at the church who were in trouble with mind-changing chemicals about his experiences. These youngsters listened to Bob so well that within four months Father Charlie found a way to pay Bob as a "youth counselor." His job was to convince teen-agers that "drugs were a bad deal."

Soon other churches were clamoring for what they began to call the Palmer Drug Abuse Program (PDAP). And they got it. The churches donated space to be used as PDAP day centers. Young people who got straight in the Palmer church's basement became their counselors.

By 1979, PDAP's thirty-nine centers in Texas and Colorado were estimated to have helped some twenty thousand drug abusers and their families. Carol Burnett, Phil Donahue, and Dinah Shore praised PDAP on nationally televised programs. Desperate parents from across the nation flew into Houston to beg for help.

Then "Sixty Minutes" produced a documentary which both praised and criticized PDAP. The organization did help young people get straight, "Sixty Minutes" said, but top echelon PDAP staff members were receiving consultants' fees from the hospitals to which addicts needing medical care were referred. "Sixty Minutes" termed the consultatory fees a conflict of interest, while PDAP called them fees for service, since PDAP counselors did work in the hospitals side by side with psychiatrists and therapists.

After "Sixty Minutes," PDAP invited the Hazelden Foundation, a nonprofit, charitable foundation specializing in substance abuse, to make a thorough evaluation of its program. Based on the Hazelden recommendations, PDAP made many changes in 1980. Edward B. Leach replaced Bob Meehan as executive director of PDAP-National. The reorganized National Board voted that no PDAP staff member should receive consultatory fees from hospitals.

PDAP has since expanded to several states. The hope is that someday this dynamic program will become available throughout the nation.

I wish to thank the seven courageous PDAP families who have given permission for me to tell their experiences in practicing "tough love." To protect their identities, I have changed their names and descriptions. These families hope that their stories will reveal new choices—and new hope—for those who must deal with a drug abuser.

Choices_____

The fly-specked clock in the jail's reception area says two A.M. The woman entering the front door could be a homemaker or an office worker—someone who believes in the PTA. She is almost clinging to her husband, a sleepy man with a puffy face. The woman's glasses cannot hide the raw dampness around her eyes. The man squints, but not from the bright neon lights. He almost pushes his wife aside to march up to the desk sergeant.

"Who the hell do I have to see about getting my son released?" he barks. He knows he is coming on strong—too strong. But how are you supposed to act when your son's been arrested?

"What's his name?" the officer asks, barely looking up from the papers on his scarred desk.

"Ted Martin," says the father, but his voice breaks.

17

He clears his throat. "Ted Martin . . . he was picked up for possession of marijuana. It's a first offense."

"Sign here," says the sergeant, pushing papers at him. Then the father pays his money.

"We'll have him in a minute," says the officer. He calls over his shoulder to the darkened hallway. "Go get Martin."

"Who?"

"Martin, Martin," yells the sergeant. At hearing his family name broadcast over the room, the father flinches. His wife fixes her eyes on the floor.

Now the parents seat themselves on a hardwood bench. They try not to stare at the long-haired boy who is vomiting on the tile floor. Beside him a middle-aged woman with a missing tooth and a man with a scar on his face yell at the bailsman. Cigar smoke mingles with the stench of unwashed bodies and the odor of disinfectant. Laughter booms from two lawyers tilting their chairs against the wall.

"Why is Ted doing this to me?" thinks the father. "I've never been in jail . . . never smoked dope . . . never done anything but work my tail off to give that kid life on a silver platter. So what does he do? Gets high . . . acts stupid . . . wrecks cars. Then he blames it all on me. The little ----! His mother has spoiled him rotten. I'll belt the hell out of him!"

Suddenly he almost doubles up. "Oh, my stomach. That's another thing that boy has done—practically given me an ulcer. Having to sit in this filthy jail doesn't help."

Ted's mother is thinking, too. "What did we do wrong? We tried to raise him right. I told him to stop

18

smoking marijuana . . . told him we're not that kind of people. In *our* family boys don't dress sloppy and let their hair grow and carry around those dirty little vials of seeds. I *know* I've been a good mother. And Ted used to be a good boy, too. Maybe if his father weren't so strict, he wouldn't be in jail. O God, I'm going to cry right here in front of everybody." She presses a damp tissue to her eyes.

Then Ted appears, his arm held by an officer with a gun in his holster. At seventeen, Ted is too slender for his height. The long hair he so adores looks almost feminine. His eyes smoulder with rage and fear.

"Now they'll be on my tail for sure. But who cares? I'm not the only one who ever got busted!" he thinks. He almost swaggers until he sees his mother. She is sobbing openly now. Suddenly Ted's eyes fill with tears. He jerks his arm away from the cop. His father grabs a handkerchief and blows his nose.

For an instant, as in one of those freeze scenes in an action movie, the three stand still. Nobody says a word, because nobody knows what to say.

Then they are walking out the door, silently getting into the car, and pulling away from the jail. Ted cowers in the back seat.

"Son, what the hell do you mean by putting your mother through all this?" his father growls.

"I'm sorry, Dad," Ted says, trying not to cry. The Martins brighten. He's never apologized before. Perhaps he has learned his lesson. Perhaps he will never touch marijuana again.

"We know you didn't mean to do it," his mother says quickly.

"But, Son, you've got to promise to get off that stuff," his father adds.

"Okay, Dad, I promise." Ted almost means it. He really didn't like being in jail, not even for an hour. But he's not sure he can go straight, either. And what would his friends think if he stopped doing dope?

No, this will not be the last time Ted is in jail. Nor will it be the last time that he and his parents ache with pain and guilt. For Ted is a drug abuser.

But Ted and his parents are not animated toys, programmed to repeat the same movements time after time in a department store window. Can't they change their actions? Can't they break the sequence?

They will try. Perhaps the parents will bribe Ted with the promise of a new stereo or a hunting trip if he stops running around with that crowd of dopers.

Or they will ground him for a month or make him clean the garage every time they find a new baggie of marijuana or a bottle of unmarked pills.

Or they will question, warn, and threaten every time he leaves the house.

Perhaps they will take him to a counselor or write a congressman and try to get the laws on illegal drug use changed.

Yes, they are willing to try. For this son was once their greatest joy. Now, like some treasured heirloom watch, he is broken. Surely they can fix him if they just try hard enough or spend the right amount of money.

Yet nothing seems to work. Ted feels guilty, all right, but he keeps on doping. He hurts, so he finds a new chemical and a new high. He lashes out at his parents, proving to himself that it doesn't matter that he is causing them anguish.

Where will Ted's story end? Perhaps in prison. Perhaps in death. *Or perhaps in a rebirth for the whole family.* For if Ted's parents gain insight into how to help a drug abuser, they can break his spiraling involvement with mind-changing chemicals. If they read this book, it is likely that they will not go to the jail at all the next time Ted is arrested.

But won't the parents then be negligent? Or uncaring? Won't they be "bad parents" if they don't rush to free their son? No, they will not. They will simply be practicing "tough love," a concept that enables the only person who can do something about his drug problems to do it. That person is Ted, the drug abuser himself.

Tough love is one of the philosophies on which the Palmer Drug Abuse Program is based. PDAP-ers know that the future for drug abusers is not hopeless. Young people who are addicted to mind-changing chemicals *can* get totally straight. They can live happy, normal lives with no dependence whatsoever on any kind of drugs.

First they must "bottom out"—reach that state of mind in which they hurt enough physically, emotionally, mentally, or spiritually to desire help. (Some of those who have reached their bottom become physical, emotional, mental, and spiritual wrecks. Others appear to be functioning "normally.")

Then they must choose to work PDAP's Twelve Steps (see page 130) and rely on the love and help of the group in order to stay off mind-changing chemicals. In this way they not only *get* sober, but they also learn to *stay* sober and find contentment by helping others recover from the effects of drugs.

Ted, however, has not yet hurt enough. He has not accepted the fact that he has a problem that he himself caused. Can PDAP help youngsters like Ted? The answer is still yes, for PDAP teaches that parents can choose to react to the drug abuser and to the events in their own lives in new ways that hasten the bottoming out process.

PDAP is for parents, too. Many have not only helped their youngsters want to get straight but they have transformed their own lives as well.

How would Ted's parents choose to act the next time Ted calls from jail if they practice tough love?

"No, Son. We love you and we want the best for you. These drugs are killing you, so we will not get you out of jail," they will say and firmly hang up the phone.

More than likely Ted will be the youngest held in the tank full of drunks and other lawbreakers that night. He may be abused. Certainly he will be terrified, humiliated, and miserable.

The next morning his parents will call a PDAP counselor, an ex-addict only slightly older than Ted, who has gotten straight in PDAP. The counselor may have hair as long as Ted's. When Ted is allowed to talk to the counselor through the bars of his cell, the counselor talks Ted's language.

"Good morning," says the counselor, grinning. "How do you like it in there? Have they changed your sheets yet?"

Ted stares glumly. He can't stand that smirk on the counselor's face. "Who the hell are you?" he asks.

"I'm a counselor with the Palmer Drug Abuse Program. Did you ever hear of it?"

"Yeah, I heard of it. It's for straight freaks."

"Right. You know, I could get you out of jail on probation if I wanted to. But I don't think I will. I'm just going to let you stay here."

Ted glares and starts to curse, but the counselor has said something about probation.

"Look, man, I want out," he says.

"Can't do it . . . not unless you can give me the usual jailhouse promises. Then I can get you out."

"What promises?"

The counselor looks Ted in the eye. "What I want to hear from you is that all this messing around with dope is over. I want to hear you say you're going to walk a line like you ain't never seen before. Now, we're willing to show you a way of life that's going to make you happy. But if you step off of it, you'll be right back in here with all your buddies."

Ted hears the snickers coming from the tank. He promises.

If PDAP's tough love sounds hard, if it grates against the sensibilities of parents and professionals who believe that good fathers and mothers don't let their children suffer, it is nonetheless a way that works for many drug abusers. PDAP has worked for those who are physically addicted to chemicals like heroin, barbiturates, and alcohol as well as for those who are psychologically addicted to marijuana and cocaine. PDAP uses no maintenance drugs. All who "make it" in PDAP learn

23

to live absolutely free of any mind-changing chemicals.

Ted doesn't need guilt-ridden parents agonizing for him at the jail. He doesn't need bribes, punishments, and excuses. What he needs is a program like PDAP, where he can experience the rebirth for which he unknowingly thirsts.

For PDAP is not only a program of tough love but it is also a way of acceptance, gentle discipline, and unconditional love as well. As soon as Ted joins PDAP, he will become a member of a warm, loving, extended family that practices a sacrament of hugs and kisses.

Parents don't need self-blame, anger, depression, and anguish, either. They can follow PDAP's Twelve Steps to find serenity and peace for themselves—and very likely a reconciliation with their drug abuser.

PDAP is not a panacea. Not every drug abuser is willing to make the sacrifices which will bring success. Not all parents are willing to make significant changes in their own lives.

To overcome habits developed over a lifetime takes patience. When we parents learn of PDAP, almost from the first we understand that we do not have to keep singing and dancing the same tune. We do not even have to experience pain and guilt if we do not wish. For we have choices.

Chapter Two

But Does It Work?

PDAP is as simple as a sewing circle, as effective as a dress factory. It is a fellowship of young people and parents who share their experience, love, and understanding so that they may solve their common problems and help others recover from the effects of mind-changing chemicals.

PDAP does not require expensive buildings or an elaborate organization. While PDAP has no religious affiliation, it makes use of rent-free space in churches for its day centers. Counselors emerge from the ranks of PDAP-ers who have become straight. The salaries of counselors and administrators come from parents and other benefactors interested in helping young people exit the drug scene.

No drug abuser or parent is ever turned away for lack of a donation, however. And no PDAP-er is ever used as a guinea pig. PDAP is not in the business of research. It requires no applications, no daily urine tests. Counselors do not even keep files on members. PDAP-ers seem to get straight just by being around one another and talking!

Counselors do not hesitate to recommend hospitalization for those who need it. They refer these youngsters to institutions which offer chemical-free treatment and employ PDAP-trained counselors to work side by side with therapists. When these patients are dismissed from the hospital, PDAP day centers offer a warm and accepting womblike atmosphere for further nurturing.

Yet many young people get straight simply by attending PDAP day centers for thirty days; and then continuing to work PDAP's Twelve Steps, which are similar to the Twelve Steps of Alcoholics Anonymous, but not identical. They continue to attend night meetings after they find jobs or return to school.

Ideally, the program works like this: parents may bring their youngsters to a PDAP center, or the courts or school district may require a drug abuser to go, or someone may walk in off the streets. The counselor determines how serious the drug problem is and urges the young person to commit to the program for at least thirty days. During that time the only requirement is the desire to live a chemical-free life.

As new members go to the center every day and attend the suggested three night meetings each week, they change in beautiful ways. Once-sullen dopers bloom into fun-loving youngsters who are able to enjoy other people without getting high.

How does the magic happen? These teen-agers break

their ties to old doping buddies and begin to model their behavior after their peers in PDAP. They attend lots of PDAP parties. They choose their sponsors. And they talk, talk, talk. In the end, they decide to work the Twelve Steps and rely on a Higher Power to change their lives.

After PDAP-ers have been sober for a month, they receive the prized monkey's fist. The knot on this braid of leather is the same one sailors tie at the end of the first line they throw ashore. PDAP-ers wear it around their necks with pride, for it represents their first contact with the dry land of sobriety after a perilous journey through the stormy waves of drug abuse.

Counselors also ask parents to attend parent meetings to learn how to cope with their drug abusers. When they do, beautiful things happen to them, too. For the first time, they are able to talk about their youngsters' doping problems in public because other parents accept them, offer encouragement, and refuse to judge.

Parents find they don't *have to* be dependent on their children for their happiness. They don't have to blame or accuse their spouses. All they have to do is relate PDAP's Twelve Steps to themselves and work to make themselves happy. As they allow their youngsters to take the responsibility for their own drug problems, they get a bonus: their youngsters improve.

Parents may cry, swear, or laugh at a PDAP meeting, secure in the knowledge that other parents will still love them. In both the young people and parent meetings, PDAP-ers are frequently seen hugging and kissing. Newcomers often balk at such an open show of affection until they learn the joy of being able to express all their feelings—including the giving and receiving of love.

For most parents and youngsters, the greatest day of all arrives when they can throw their arms around each other and say, "I love you," and mean it.

Even parents whose children have not yet bottomed out enough to come to PDAP often become active members. Why? They learn to find happiness in circumstances that have crushed others.

How does PDAP work? Ordinary people help one another. In a typical PDAP parent meeting, discussions cover such topics as the Twelve Steps, honesty, anger, guilt, and tough love. All those present share their experiences and tell how they have solved problems. Parents also attend Round Robins—a day-long feast of meetings—which can result in instant growth.

As participants listen to others, they are often struck by the similarity of feelings, frustrations, failures, and successes which they have experienced. As they hear how others have overcome fear, anger, depression, or self-pity, they are free to choose new ways of modeling their own behavior.

Every parent who has "made it" in PDAP has a dramatic story of self-change to tell. The next seven chapters will describe how seven families did succeed in PDAP. The names are fictitious, but the people, the feelings, the struggles, and the victories are real.

The Family That Had Everything Under Control_____

When George and Liz bought a new house, they accepted all its amenities as their due, for they felt they were good parents, typical upper middle-class Americans. Why shouldn't they own four bedrooms, a den, a pleasant yard with a creek—and four children over whom they had absolute control?

Though the neighborhood was expensive, a wooded slope near the house was nicknamed "Hippie Hill," because teen-agers often made a racket there with their all-night drinking and pill popping parties.

"You'd better watch your children and keep them away from that place," Liz's mother warned. But George and Liz only laughed. In the communities in which they had grown up, their families had been leaders. Both thought dopers the lowest possible form of humanity.

"I felt that I was a real good mother," remembers Liz. "I thought we were raising the children right and that they would grow up without any problems." Both she and George were committed to their marriage and to their role as parents. They saw to it that the kids were in Indian Guides, Cub Scouts, webelos, and YMCA baseball and football.

When their oldest son, Paul, made some Fs in junior high, George and Liz simply warned him that he would need good grades if he wanted to be a doctor. Sure enough, Paul's grades improved. They had always expected Paul to do well, and he did. Paul even got himself up early every morning to throw a paper route all by himself. Yes, he was a good boy, and everything was under control.

The first time they knew that Paul had used drugs was when he was twelve. One Saturday morning as the family prepared for an outing to the lake, Paul didn't seem to be able to wake up. He mumbled that he felt sick. George suggested he nap in the car on the trip out. Paul slept, all right. Even after they arrived he stayed in the cabin, groggy all day. Not until the next morning did he recover enough energy to go swimming.

When the family returned, the mother of one of Paul's friends telephoned. She told Liz that Paul had been with her own son and another friend when they sneaked a bottle of prescription barbiturates out of her medicine cabinet. The other boys had swallowed so many pills that they had to have their stomachs pumped to keep them from dying. When confronted with this information, Paul confessed that he too had taken some pills.

"But I didn't take as many as they wanted me to," he said. He promised not to do such a dangerous thing again.

Not long afterward when Liz did the laundry, she found some hand-rolled cigarettes in Paul's jeans. The filler looked more like dried spices than tobacco. Could this be marijuana? The thought chilled her.

"Sure, that's pot," said Paul. "But it's not mine. It belongs to a friend."

But soon Paul began coming home in a drunken state, though his breath bore no scent of alcohol. He had to admit he was smoking pot. Each time he promised never to do it again. The family pediatrician consoled them.

"Paul may just sample marijuana, and that will be the end of it," he said.

Again and again they found more pot around the house. Now when George and Liz tried to tell Paul that marijuana was dangerous and illegal, Paul began to retort, "There isn't anything wrong with pot." Or, "I'm really not into it very much. My friends are, but I'm not."

George and Liz were scared. They knew that good people couldn't go around with bad ones without having some of the unacceptable behavior rub off on them. And Paul's friends looked pretty bad, with their long hair and dirty jeans. Later George and Liz were to realize that Paul's appearance was changing drastically, too. But he became dirty, disheveled, and sickly looking so gradually that they didn't realize how bad he was. Besides, they didn't want to believe it. Still, they tried very hard to persuade him to change his ways.

"We would sit Paul down and talk to him,"

remembers Liz. "And we thought we were communicating with him. But what we were actually doing was laying down the law to him. *We* talked but he didn't.

"At the time, we felt that as parents we had the responsibility to know everything Paul thought and everything he did. We thought that if we knew all, we could control all. This attitude was part of our problem, which we didn't then recognize."

George and Liz sometimes considered taking Paul to a minister for counseling, but they hadn't been active in their church for a long time. God hadn't seemed too important before Paul started smoking dope. Could it be that God was punishing them now by making all this happen? They felt so guilty that they couldn't bring themselves to face the minister.

Mostly what they did was worry—and feel a lot of resentment. Liz knew that George had done a lot of Scouting with Paul, but still she felt like saying to him, "If you had done more, Paul would not be having this problem. We would be a tighter family unit." She didn't, though. She held her tongue and smoldered inside. Instead, when George returned from work every day she would meet him at the door with complaints about Paul's behavior, forcing George to discipline the boy.

When Paul turned sixteen, he wanted to buy a car with the four hundred dollars he had saved. George and Liz thought that if Paul had wheels to carry him away fom the neighborhood, he would get away from that dirty, long-haired crowd and find new friends. So they added enough to the four hundred dollars to enable him to buy a car.

Instead, Paul's doping got worse. One night they

looked outside and saw him sitting in the car with the lights on. The car reeked with the smell of pot. Paul was stoned. They grounded him for a week. But by now Paul was taller than they. When he wanted to leave the house he simply pushed his mother aside and left while she yelled helplessly at him.

George and Liz lectured. They pleaded. They cried. There were mortifying incidents with friends when no one could cover up the fact that Paul was either high or acting in a bizarre manner.

Then one morning, when Paul was in the shower, his father yelled to him that he was going to move the boy's car out of the driveway.

"No, don't do that, I'll move it," Paul yelled back. George was suspicious. He ran out and started to unlock the car. Suddenly something hit him from behind and he found himself knocked sprawling with his glasses flying off his nose. Looking up, he saw Paul, stark naked except for a towel, jumping into the car. Anger exploded in George and he came up shouting. "If you don't get out of that car, I'll tear you to pieces," he said.

Paul grabbed a baggie of pot and shot out of the car. Right there in front of the whole neighborhood, George went after Paul with his fists. Dropping the towel, Paul raced for the creek with George fast behind. But the boy got away.

When George returned to the house panting and red-faced, he saw his wife, his daughters, and his daughters' friends watching.

"I felt," said Liz, "that I was watching a tragic thing happen and there was nothing I could do about it. It was like Paul's dope was the most important thing in the world to him."

When Paul sneaked back into the house, George followed him upstairs. They fought some more.

Finally George yelled, "Just get your clothes and get out of here." But after Paul left, George was filled with remorse. Paul had been a good son, and now he seemed to be deeply in trouble with marijuana. As a father, shouldn't he be trying to help? He was sure that this time he could talk some sense into the boy. So he searched Paul out and took him to a tavern for a man-to-man talk over a beer.

"I'm sorry for what I did," Paul said. But he didn't volunteer to give back the pot. It stayed hidden somewhere around the creek.

Meanwhile, Liz was phoning her pediatrician and insisting he had to do something about Paul. When the doctor suggested Alcoholics Anonymous, she almost felt sick at her stomach. But she made herself phone. AA referred her to PDAP.

Liz knew nothing about PDAP, but she was glad to know there was some organization that might help Paul. The next day she went to the PDAP center in the basement of a church. Somehow she thought she was taking Paul to see the church's youth minister, but the counselor didn't look like a preacher. He looked very much like Paul's long-haired friends. Right away he told her he was an ex-addict.

Liz didn't quite trust the counselor, yet she had the feeling that he knew all there was to know about her son. It was uncanny. It was almost as if he could see all the things that had been happening at her house.

"I'd like you to make a thirty-day commitment to the program," the counselor told both Liz and Paul. "There's a meeting tonight. I think you both should go." A reluctant Paul went to his first PDAP meeting that night. Liz persuaded George to go with her to the parent group. As George and Liz listened to the other mothers and fathers, they felt a certain amount of smugness. Some of these parents freely shared the fact that they themselves had had a drinking problem. Others were divorced. It was natural that their children should have drug habits.

But why did Paul have a problem? After all, they'd stayed married seventeen years, much longer than many of their friends. They had been good parents who gave plenty of guidance and direction to their children. They didn't have a serious drinking problem, either. So what had gone wrong?

No, they didn't believe they belonged in a drug abuse program. But they were determined to stick it out for thirty days for Paul's sake. At the end of the month, they figured that Paul would be "cured." But the counselor had told Liz something that really bothered her.

"Drugs are like an iceberg," he had said. "They're the little part at the top that shows. You can't see all the rest of the problem." Liz didn't want to believe that Paul had serious problems. He had always been an achiever.

After thirty days, George and Liz expected Paul to receive a monkey's fist. But he did not.

"Paul has never stopped smoking pot," explained the counselor. "He's been high at just about every meeting." George and Liz could hardly believe it. After all, they had seen some improvement in Paul's behavior.

Had he been high constantly and they hadn't recognized the symptoms?

The counselor said that the only way Paul was going to get off marijuana was to go to a hospital that specialized in working with drug abusers. He recommended one in Houston which permitted PDAP counselors to work side by side with psychiatrists and therapists.

"You could tell Paul he has the choice of either going to the Houston hospital or getting out of your house," he said. George and Liz were so dismayed to hear that Paul was still getting high that they decided to give the boy that choice—even though they knew practically nothing about the hospital's method of treatment.

The next day George withdrew his son from school. When Paul came home, he and Liz told him his choices. Paul threw a book across the room.

"You mother-fuckers!" Paul shouted. "You're nothing but a bunch of crazy fanatics, you and your PDAP. Hell, no. I won't go to any hospital. I'll be glad to leave this nutty house."

He ran upstairs, grabbed some clothes and his marijuana. He lit up in front of his parents, shot a middle finger at them, and stomped out of the house. They heard his car roar out of the driveway.

George and Liz stared at each other. What had they done? They had been positive that Paul would cooperate. Now he had left and they couldn't back down. They were scared and sweaty-handed. Liz burst into tears. George phoned the counselor.

"Don't go running after him," the counselor said. "Let him take the responsibility for his actions."

"But what will he do? Where will he go?"

"That's up to him to make the choice," said the counselor. "You can help him make the right choice faster if you tell him you don't want to see him until he goes to PDAP. Don't give him money or any kind of help. Don't pad his corners and make it easy for him to go on doping."

Soon George and Liz learned that Paul had moved in with the grandmother of a doping buddy named Ken. Ken's father was giving the boys money.

"They're just sowing some wild oats," he told George. "Don't worry. This will all be over soon."

But the boys were too wild for the grandmother. Soon the boys had an apartment of their own and after-school jobs. George and Liz were depressed.

"We felt that without our control Paul would be ten times worse off. What if he got drunk and tried to drive that old car?" thought George. "What if he got into harder drugs?" Each night they imagined worse horrors.

Up until this point, George and Liz had not been taking the PDAP parent meetings too seriously. Now they gave them top priority. When Liz cried, other parents comforted her. When George worried, other fathers reminded him to live one day at a time. Somehow, they always felt better after attending the meetings.

"We would go to a meeting and get pumped up for two to three days. Then we would sink back into our depression. The only thing that helped was to go to another meeting," George remembers.

Now the Serenity Prayer, repeated at each meeting, began to mean something to them: "God grant me the serenity to accept the things I cannot change, the courage to change the things I can, and the wisdom to know the difference."

George and Liz knew they could not change Paul. None of the things they had done to control him had made any difference in the amount of pot he smoked. So now they worked at accepting their powerlessness. Other parents told them they could turn Paul over to God's care. Even though they didn't know much about praying, they tried it and they felt better.

Still other parents told them that while they needed to accept the fact that they couldn't change Paul, they *could* work to change themselves. They said that George and Liz could choose to be happy even with their son on the streets. They didn't really see how they could do that, but they tried. They went to meetings. They talked about their feelings. They began to achieve some serenity.

When Paul called and invited them to come to his apartment, Liz had enough serenity to say, "We love you, Paul. That's why we are allowing you to do whatever you need to do. But please don't call us. Call the PDAP counselor if you want to talk to somebody."

After she hung up, Liz cried. But she knew that the counselor was right. The only way Paul could be helped was for him to realize that he was responsible for his own actions. He needed to "bottom out" and make the decision to work the PDAP program on his own.

Thanksgiving came and went without their seeing Paul. George couldn't stand it. On the Sunday after the holiday, he began to wonder if the counselor was wrong. He decided to try one more time to talk some sense into the boy. Without telling Liz, he slipped out of the house and went to his son's apartment. There he found Paul, Ken, and their friends lying on couches. The floor was littered with beer and whiskey bottles. The boys were dead drunk.

George took one look and backed out the door. The PDAP counselor had been right. Nothing he could say to the boys was going to change them.

With more holidays coming, George and Liz were really down. They made plans to visit Liz's parents on Christmas Day. They didn't invite Paul, not even when he phoned and hinted for an invitation.

Early on Christmas morning, as they got ready to drive to the grandparents' house, Liz found a Christmas present sitting on the front porch. It was from Paul, to the whole family. They opened it with tears rolling down their faces.

At Christmas dinner, George and Liz told their relatives that Paul had gone on a skiing trip for the holidays. But Liz's father was very disappointed. He was facing a terminal illness and he wanted to see his oldest grandson. During the next week, he kept phoning. Finally, George and Liz had to tell him that Paul had a drug problem. They told him all about PDAP and the choices they had given Paul. Grandpa was horrified.

"If I were physically able, I would come over and stay with Paul myself until he got over his drug problem," he said.

"How would you get him over it?" Liz asked.

"Why, if I had to, I would tie him to the bed until he was well. This is no way to treat the boy."

The grandparents just couldn't understand that there

was more to getting straight than getting sober. Everything they said made George and Liz feel guilty.

"If you'd brought him up like we brought you up, then you wouldn't be having all this trouble," they as much as said. Soon they were padding Paul's corners with gifts of clothing and a new watch.

"How will he ever bottom out like this?" Liz asked the counselor.

"You could give Paul the choice of going to the Houston hospital or being committed to the state hospital. Tell him he is still sixteen and you can phone the police and have him committed there," he said.

Given this ultimatum, a very hostile Paul went to see the counselor. While he was there, George slipped into the church's chapel.

"I had been brought up in the church, but when I got to be an adult, I thought I didn't need a Higher Power anymore. But here I was, down on my knees at the altar. I knew that I didn't deserve help, but Paul did. I asked God, if he was really there, to help Paul make the decision to go to Houston."

When George returned to the PDAP office, the counselor handed him the phone.

"Paul won't go. You'll have to call the police," he said. Wearily George started to dial. Then Paul said in a very small voice, "I'll go."

All the way to Houston it was like having a wild animal in the car. Paul cursed and kicked the seat. He said that his parents were fanatics who were ruining his life. George and Liz were so afraid he would jump out that they didn't stop once.

Finally they stood in the hospital and watched a nurse

take Paul to an elevator that had to be unlocked. And suddenly they wondered what they had done. On the recommendation of a counselor who was an ex-addict, not a doctor, they had signed their son into the locked ward of a strange hospital in another city for thirty days. Paul had accused them of being fanatics. Had he been right?

Back home they went to parent meetings to bolster their morale. Two weeks later Paul phoned them. He sounded just as hostile as ever. He wanted them to use the money from his last paycheck to cover the rent on his apartment because he was planning to come right back.

In another two weeks, George and Liz were allowed to visit Paul. As they took the locked elevator to Paul's floor, they were filled with dread and guilt. But when the door opened, they saw a pleasant place full of young people who were laughing and talking. No one looked crazy.

Then they saw Paul. He seemed strangely different. For one thing, he was smiling at them. And for another, he looked healthy. With a shock they realized he hadn't looked that way for years.

Now Paul was bounding across the room. He was throwing his arms around them both. They could feel his arms tightening around them.

"Mom . . . Dad . . . I love you," he said. George and Liz froze for an instant. Then they started to sob. They cried so hard they had to go out into the hall. They went to the rest rooms and washed their faces and sat in the car and cried some more.

"We just couldn't get control of ourselves," George remembers. "It was all such a relief. We were so happy!

The son we hadn't had for two or three years was back to normal."

In three more weeks, Paul was ready to leave the hospital and George and Liz were apprehensive. Certainly Paul seemed changed, but what would happen when he came home?

"Just take it easy," said the counselor. "Don't put any pressure on him. Let him get active with the other PDAP-ers here at the day center. Then maybe he can think about going back to school."

But Paul wanted to return to school and get his old job back immediately. When he did, his old buddy, Ken, came back, too. Ken persuaded Paul to trade his car plus a hundred dollars for a friend's motorcycle.

George knew that Paul would be rooked if he fell for that deal. Besides, both he and Liz were scared to death of motorcycles. But the PDAP counselor told George that Paul needed to make his own decisions. Paul needed to take the consequences of his acts without George's protecting him. So George let his son make the foolish trade.

The very first night Paul had the motorcycle, he went out with Ken and got high! While the counselor had told George and Liz that Paul might have a slip, both parents felt icy fear. By now Paul had told them that in the past he had tried a lot more mind-changing chemicals than marijuana. He had sampled LSD, shot and sniffed cocaine, and swallowed all kinds of pills. Since he had been much deeper into drugs than they had ever imagined, what would happen if he went back to doping again?

It took a lot of tough love to do what the counselor

advised, but they did it. When Paul came in for supper, they told him he couldn't come home till he had seen the counselor. Paul roared off on his motorcycle and didn't come home that night.

Later they learned that he had spent the night with the counselor and was back in PDAP the next day. But that twenty-four hours of frantic worry was enough for both George and Liz to realize that they had not worked the Twelve Steps sufficiently.

"All the time we'd been in PDAP I had thought that Paul certainly needed every one of those Twelve Steps," says George. "They were for him, not me. Finally some of the words I'd heard at the meetings began to soak in. I started working on my own program."

George and Liz both got a sponsor—another PDAP parent with whom they could share their feelings and ask to look at their problems objectively. They began a Step study. They found they were already practicing Step One—accepting the fact that a part of their lives had become unmanageable because of the mind-changing chemicals. And Step Two was easy, because they had already found it necessary to "stick with winners." Certainly the people who had insisted on padding Paul's corners had been losers for them. The PDAP parents who helped had been winners.

But for George, Steps Three and Four were stumbling blocks. In these Steps he was to realize that there was a Higher Power who could help restore him to sanity. He was to make a decision to turn his will and life over to the care of God as he understood him.

Not until he went to a Round Robin and heard others

tell about how they understood God could he overcome his doubts about a Higher Power.

"As a child I'd been taught that God would get you if you were bad. He could hate you and make evil things happen to you. But at the Round Robin I heard others saying that God was a friend, a loving God, no matter what you did. I didn't have to be perfect.

"And I also learned that Step Four didn't say you had to turn your whole life over to God. I didn't feel capable of doing that. The step just said I had to be *willing* to do it. Well, I was willing," he said.

Liz also began to work the Twelve Steps. She discovered how helpful it was to accept her powerlessness over Paul and other people.

During this time, her father was dying. The Steps helped her cope. Because she was powerless, she didn't have to try to make him understand Paul's problem. She could forgive him and accept him. "I had never been able to hug or kiss my father, but now I could do that. I told him I loved him before he died," she said.

Eventually George and Liz got all their children involved in PDAP. Their second son, Al, had no drug problem, but he had always seemed to feel incompetent in everything. In PDAP he gained confidence as George and Liz let him be responsible for his own grades.

After three years in PDAP, Paul became a counselor. Now the three younger children use the Twelve Steps in their own lives.

"There's more laughter and freedom in our house now," says George. "As Liz and I improved our relationship, the whole family seemed to calm down.

The girls are much more open, happier, and freer. They can share with us where they're at in their lives.

"The girls are now in junior high and we can see them working their own program, reaching out, knowing that God is for them. They make their self-esteem lists. They have their friends. We don't ever have to wait up all night till they come in, because we know they are being responsible for themselves. When they are out with PDAP-ers, we know they are having good, clean fun."

Only by seriously working the Twelve Steps did the family get to this point. Letting Paul buy the motorcycle was the first in a continuing series of revelations. By taking the consequences of his act, Paul learned a lesson from the motorcycle incident that his parents could never have taught him. Every time he rode his machine in the rain, he got soaked. It was always breaking, too. Eventually he sold the thing and lost his hundred-dollar investment. George and Liz began to realize that by trying to control everything their children did, they had actually caused a lot of friction.

"We used to have a lot of rules. The kids had to make good grades. I needed to know where they were and they had to be home at a certain time. Their rooms had to be clean," remembers Liz. "They even had to spend their allowance like I thought they should. I was telling them, 'As long as you're doing what *I* want you to, you're being responsible.' I did not see that I was not giving them the freedom to develop rules for themselves."

"Now we give Al and the girls an allowance each week. In return they are to empty the trash and be responsible for taking care of their own rooms, their own space. Everybody is to clean up his or her own mess wherever it is made.

"Now when the kids don't take out the trash, they don't get their allowances. We don't say much about it. We just don't give the money. In the past we would have made excuses and given it to them anyway."

Both George and Liz have learned the value of praising rather than criticizing.

"It used to be that when the kids brought home their report cards, we would praise them for making an A and nothing else. Even if they made a 91 on a test, we would point out how they should have made a 96 or 97. We put down even the good grades! We withheld praise in many areas in which they did do well. We just assumed they would know they did well even if we said nothing," says Liz.

"Now I know how psychologically damaging criticism is. I am working on letting my children—and other people, too—know how neat they are when they do something well. By being very open with the kids in how I feel and in admitting my own mistakes, I have found my children becoming more open in their communication with me. I can let them make mistakes and learn."

George is also working to let his children take control of their own lives. "I used to have to wake everybody in the morning and then get upset because they wouldn't get up," he says. "Now I hear their alarm clocks waking me up. They get themselves ready for school. I no longer have to tell them how to do everything as if they were little children. They can feel proud and self-reliant.

"When someone breaks the rules or does something that needs to be changed, we now have a family meeting.

If the children are leaving a mess in the den, rather than insisting they do things our way, we tell them they're not being responsible, they're not working their programs.

"What is most important, though, is that I no longer feel it is my duty to teach them responsibility. A hug around the neck, a loving pat gets ten times more results than yelling and screaming. I'm not saying we don't get mad at one another. We do. We all have our slips. Sometimes when Al gets bad grades, I start worrying that he's going to turn out a bum. I carry my worry around with me awhile and get myself all messed up, and finally I start working my program again. I leave him alone, and sure enough he turns out all right. Things get back on an even keel," says George.

But how did the Twelve Steps so change the way Liz and George are living? Both made a "searching and fearless moral inventory" of themselves (Step Five). They shared it with another human being and with God (Step Six), and then became willing to allow their Higher Power to help them change their way of life (Step Seven). Then they made amends to those they had hurt (Steps Eight and Nine) and learned to continue to admit their wrongs at the time they happened (Step Ten). Finally they sought closer contact with God through prayer and meditation (Step Eleven) and tried to carry their love and understanding to others (Step Twelve).

George says, "After doing the inventory, I was able to find something about myself that I wanted to change. One was that I was overweight. In six months I lost forty pounds simply by turning over to God my desire to snack.

"When I learned to pray every morning and turn my

life over to God, I began arriving at work feeling good. I could sleep at night. All my nervous stomach problems went away.

"I found that the more I helped others, the better off I became. Certainly there's been a great change in my relationship with Liz. We didn't know how good our marriage could be until we learned to share our true feelings."

Liz says, "We used to play a lot of games in our marriage. I always assumed that George was responsible for my happiness, even though I never told him what I wanted. In turn, I felt it was my duty to keep him happy, too. We both punished each other a lot for not filling each other's needs.

"Also, I was afraid to let George know when I was feeling insecure or down, because I was afraid he would use this knowledge to hurt me deeply. Now I know we are both committed to love each other and I can trust him."

When the time came for Paul to move out to his own apartment, his parents recognized that it would be good for him to take the responsibility for his own life.

"But when Paul came and said, 'I am moving on Tuesday,' I had all these wild feelings," says Liz. "My head said, 'Yes, that will be good for you,' but my gut said, 'I do not want you to go. I want to be with you.'

"But finally I realized this attitude was just another way of wanting Paul to 'make' me happy. I had to go back and work the Steps, and then I realized that I did not have to see him every day to love him. I could love him no matter where he was."

After Paul became a PDAP counselor, he was

transferred to another city. Liz is glad that she does not feel she has to try to live through others. She has her own life to live, and so does Paul.

George and Liz learned that trying to control children doesn't work. By giving them freedom to take the responsibility for their own lives, they found a more loving way to live for themselves.

Chapter Four

The Family That Didn't Give Up

Lisa was an only child. Up until the time she was thirteen, her parents thought they had an idyllic family. They could have easily passed for the complacent parents in a television comedy.

Of course, Lisa's parents, Dot and Bart, each had some gnawing anxieties which they didn't discuss. Bart kept getting angry for no apparent reason. Dot suffered frequent ulcer-like attacks for which the doctor could find no physical reason.

But they had a lovely home. They read the right books. They went to good plays from time to time. Both Bart and Dot had interesting careers. No doubt about it, they had bettered themselves far beyond their own parents' expectations.

While they were living in Pennsylvania, thirteen-year-old Lisa started running around with a wild group of teen-agers. She dated some rough-looking boys who were much too old for her. She stole money from her parents and used it to buy friendships.

When Bart received a job offer from Texas, he and Dot were delighted that Lisa was going to escape the bad influence of that bunch of no-goods. For about six months after the move, Lisa's grades improved. Her new friends looked like "good girls." But then Lisa's hostility returned. Twice when Dot was only ten minutes late coming home from work, Lisa kicked in the door to the house rather than wait.

Whenever Lisa misbehaved, Dot would argue and scold. But Bart would avoid unpleasantness by saying he had to work. Even if an argument began at 10 P.M., Bart would leave and escape to the office.

Dot didn't say anything to Bart, but she resented having to discipline Lisa by herself. Her irritation festered. Soon she found herself flying into real tantrums over nothing at all. If Bart so much as forgot to put a new roll of toilet paper on the rack when he used the last sheet, she would rage at him.

Bart was angry, too. Sometimes he became so furious at Dot's sullenness and Lisa's hostility, that he would knock the furniture around. Both parents felt their anger was all due to Lisa's action. They made sick jokes with her.

"We're going to chain you to the bed to keep you out of trouble," they would tease. Or they would threaten, "We'll buy you a bus ticket to anywhere you want to go if you promise never to come home." The kidding didn't mask their real feelings very well.

"I felt an icy wall of resentment and anger toward

Lisa," Dot said. "We had given her so many good things in life, and she just seemed to want to throw them all away. Now I know that part of my resentment stemmed from the fact that her misbehavior made me feel that I hadn't done a good enough job of being a parent. I felt guilty."

Lisa went from bad to worse. One day she attended a rock concert with her girl friend and didn't come home. Her friend said Lisa had left the concert with a strange boy. Dot became almost hysterical. Bart phoned the police. The officers called every friend in Lisa's address book, but could find no one who knew where Lisa was. Neighbors used CB radios trying to trace her path. Throughout the long night, no one slept.

The next afternoon Lisa was found at the lake, with a boy she had known a long time. Dot and Bart fired questions at her. But Lisa was evasive.

"Nothing happened. Don't worry about it," was all she would say. Dot and Bart were so exhausted, so drained, and so confused that they let Lisa go to her room with only a scolding. But then they stared at each other with the same fear and hurt in their eyes.

"Maybe Lisa is mentally ill," they said. But they did nothing. A week later Lisa ran away again. Her parents suffered the same agony.

When they found Lisa this time, Dot wasted no time in setting up an appointment with a psychiatrist. She took Lisa to work with her on the day of the appointment. Lisa spent the morning talking to some of the younger employees whom Dot managed and then ran away that afternoon. This time Dot didn't bother to look for her. She let her daughter return on her own.

Meanwhile, one of the younger employees told Dot that Lisa was on drugs.

Dot couldn't believe it. She knew that Lisa's nice-looking friends were a bit wild, because when the police used Lisa's address book, they recognized every name. But she didn't know the friends were dopers. That night she confronted Lisa.

"How long have you been doping, Lisa?" she asked.

Dot knew that Lisa had a habit of conning. The girl could look straight at her mother and fabricate a lie that seemed so reasonable Dot always half believed her. But this time Lisa told the truth. She had been on drugs for several months.

Somehow Dot got Lisa to go to the PDAP counselor. He suggested that Lisa stay in school and arranged for her to leave early every afternoon so she could be at the PDAP day center from two to four. During the thirty days, Lisa was not to use any mind-changing chemicals. She was to "stick with winners" in PDAP and avoid her old doping buddies.

Dot and Bart made a thirty-day commitment to attend parent meetings, too. They promised they would not try to enforce any rules about curfews or smoking, or anything else that was causing friction with Lisa.

"If you have any problems with her, just call me and turn them over to me," said the counselor.

What a relief! That's exactly what they did. Listen to what Dot says about her first days in PDAP.

"I'd always been a justifier and an explainer when I had to refuse Lisa permission for something. She would always ask why, and I would give her a very thorough, rational explanation. Then she would look at me, smile, and say, 'Well, why can't I?' We would repeat this procedure two or three times until finally I would get mad and say, 'Forget it, I'm the mother and I say no,' or I would give in.

"One of the first things I learned in PDAP was not to argue when I meant no, but just to say, 'I'm not willing to do so and so.' And that was the end of it. If Lisa didn't like it, she could discuss it with the counselor. At first Lisa would try to argue, but soon she accepted my 'I'm not willing' as meaning there was no possible argument.

"In fact, after an initial two weeks when Lisa expressed resentment about PDAP, she began to work the program very willingly. She became a sponsor to another member almost right away. And she really wanted to help the newcomers. But she was still negative at home and making poor grades at school.

"Bart and I both began to work hard at releasing the angry feeling we had toward Lisa. We wanted to be able to love her, to really care about her, to separate her bad behavior from herself as a person. We were able finally to let go of some of those angers by working the first Four Steps. Learning to let go was going to make a whole lot of difference in the way I would be able to react toward what happened later on," said Dot.

After being sober for about six weeks, Lisa began using drugs secretly. When confronted by the counselor, Lisa insisted she hadn't been doping. The counselor had to kick her out of PDAP. If he let her stay in, she might influence others, especially new people, to get high.

By this time Dot and Bart realized that they would be padding Lisa's corners if they let her come home. They had to give her the chance to accept the consequences of her acts. If they tried to protect her, they would be putting a serious obstacle in her goal of a straight life. Lisa had made her choice. She would have to be out on the streets, on her own.

Lisa came home, packed three sacks with dirty jeans, and promised to ask to rejoin PDAP the next week. But she didn't.

"I was in the pits," remembers Dot. "I thought, here's my blonde, blue-eyed baby who is only fifteen and doesn't know much about protecting herself from the wrong kind of men. Other parents who had had kids on the street reminded me that if I went looking for her and invited her to come home I would be making it just that much easier for her to continue to dope. Rationally I knew this was true, but I just couldn't deal with my feelings. Other parents told me to turn her over to God and let him be responsible for her, but I couldn't seem to do it. I was really hurting."

At a Round Robin meeting on willingness, Dot heard someone say, "God helps those who let him do his work himself."

"It dawned on me that I had been trying to do God's work for him all my life. By trying to take over God's role in 'making' Lisa get straight, I was practicing self-will and putting one more obstacle in God's way. I decided I would really turn Lisa over to God and let him work *his* will for her, not mine. Immediately I felt better.

"When I got home, one of Lisa's friends called and told me a pitiful story about how Lisa had been sleeping in the park all week. Before the meeting, this phone call would have had one sure result: I would have told Lisa's friend that I wanted Lisa to come home. Now, all I did was say, 'Awww, poor Lisa,' in a tone of amusement and acceptance.''

"Then the friend said, 'Well, would you like to know where you can reach Lisa if you want her?' I answered, 'No, I really don't want to know.'

"I have to admit that I had to keep turning Lisa over to God all the time, because I still had a lot of fear. I would put Lisa in his hands as many as a hundred times as I drove to work. But finally I would get a real serenity, even when I was afraid that bad things were happening to her and I was very shaken inside.

"After two weeks I was thrilled when Lisa phoned and said that she was going to have an interview with all the PDAP counselors who would make the decision about whether to let her come back into the program. But a few hours later I got another call from her. She was crying.

"'They're cruel! They won't let me back in,' she said.

"I learned later that the counselor could tell that Lisa wanted back in PDAP just so she could come home. She had no real intention of staying straight. But as I was talking to her on the phone I had to fight back the impulse to sympathize with her. It seemed to me that Lisa was showing a lot of maturity by asking to come back to PDAP. However, I also had faith in PDAP. I was determined to go along with whatever the counselors said. If they thought Lisa needed more willingness to work the program, then she probably did. I would be padding her corners if I let her come back home.

"Only a week later, Lisa went back to the counselors.

This time she was willing to do anything they asked of her. She was allowed back into PDAP," says Dot.

PDAP recommended that Lisa go to the hospital. She spent seven weeks there and emerged a superstar, a real leader in PDAP. But right after Christmas, she and another girl "slipped" again. They went out doping for two days before a truant officer found them.

This time Lisa freely admitted to the PDAP counselor that she had slipped. Because she had an honest and willing attitude, the counselor let her stay in PDAP. By March she was making so much progress that the counselor appointed her to the steering committee. Not only was this position a high honor, but as she helped lead the other teen-agers, Lisa would be an example to the new members.

At home, however, Lisa was still uncooperative about helping with chores or cleaning her room. Her grades weren't very good either. Dot and Bart tried practicing the Twelve Steps and managed to accept this behavior because they recognized that Lisa was "just that way." Soon, however, they found money disappearing from their pocketbooks. Bart discovered bills coming in on charge cards that neither he nor Dot had used. The counselor decided to remove Lisa from the steering committee but allow her to keep going to PDAP.

"Just treat Lisa as if she has a terminal illness that she really can't help," he said. "Accept and trust her."

But the bad behavior continued. Dot and Bart couldn't let go of their anger.

"She's just ripping us off," they told each other. Every night Bart and Lisa had a big fight. Finally Bart took her to the counselor.

"I'm willing to do anything to help her get well. But she can't live at home," he said. The counselor found her another PDAP family with whom to live. That relationship lasted only two weeks, because Lisa promptly stole fifty dollars from her foster family.

At that point Lisa's sponsor pressed her to take a personal inventory as a means of overcoming her bad behavior. Lisa wrote about her past, but she didn't go into depth on anything. She just couldn't be serious or give her life any deep thought. Now her parents realize that Lisa was practicing a form of denial for a very good reason that no one, not even she, was to recognize for several more months. At the time she just seemed to be flippant and irresponsible.

As soon as school let out in June, Lisa went back on the streets on her own. Because Bart and Dot had been working their own Twelve-Step programs for a year, they could face Lisa's being out with more detachment this time. When Lisa went to see Bart at his office, he would simply tell her he did not want to see her unless she went to PDAP. When Lisa phoned her mother, Dot didn't press her to come back into the program.

"The first time she was on the streets, I always asked God not to let her suffer any more than he had to in order for her to get well. This time I was praying to God to let her have all the pain there was. I felt that only by really hurting could she bottom out and want to get straight badly enough to work at it. If she had to suffer to reach that point, that was what I wanted, and the sooner the better," Dot said.

"This time I felt very comfortable, very detached. I felt it was really not my part to do anything about Lisa. I felt that God would take care of her. And it was really necessary for her to be out on the street.

"I also felt at this point that I loved her. Lisa and I had never been close, but now I felt closer than before."

When Lisa returned to PDAP, she spent three weeks with another PDAP family. But her attitude toward her parents was very bad. The counselors gave her a choice: either go back to the hospital or leave the program. Lisa hit the streets again.

Within a week Lisa was phoning every three or four days and asking to come home. Dot and Bart always said no, not unless she was willing to return to the hospital.

Finally one night Lisa called. She sounded terrified.

"I want to come home. Please come and get me!" she begged.

"Not unless you're willing to go to the hospital," replied Bart. He and Dot never knew what had happened to make Lisa change, but this time she was willing. They went to get her.

After nine weeks in the hospital Lisa came home a different person. A lot of the "games" she had been playing with her parents were a thing of the past.

"Lisa no longer conned, or played 'give me' or 'I've gotta have' or sulked. If she asked for money and Bart gave her only a dollar, she accepted the fact that that was all he had to give at the time," said Dot.

Dot and Bart also grew a lot while Lisa was in the hospital. One day Bart got a call at work from Lisa. She told him the hospital therapist had asked her to confront him about something that had been bothering her a long time. It was a problem she had never revealed to anyone before. Listen to what Bart has to say about it:

"I had been playing a sexual game on Lisa for at least ten years, but I never told anyone about it, and neither did she. When I would tell Lisa good night, I would fondle her. I don't know why I did it. I just did it. When Lisa phoned, she demanded that I stop or she would take some other action. I agreed.

"Actually I had known that these sexual games were a problem for me and for Lisa too. In PDAP I had tried to take a personal inventory. But I hadn't been honest with myself. I had admitted everything I disliked about myself, except the fondling. My inventory was far from being thorough. So after I shared it with another person, I didn't feel very good. In fact I was angry—angrier than I had ever been before.

"After Lisa confronted me, I didn't know what to do , and I wasn't really willing to do anything on my own. But finally the PDAP counselor called me in and urged me to get professional help. Since then I've been seeing a psychiatrist and he is helping me see a lot of reasons why I related to Lisa that way. I can see now that I converted a lot of fear and guilt into anger. I lived that way for a long time. I would take that anger out on others.

"I still have a long way to go, but I'm working on my problems. I feel that things will get better," Bart said.

Now that Lisa is sixteen and working her program, Bart realizes that for the first time in years he is really enjoying having her at home.

After Lisa returned from her second hospital stay, she went to the PDAP day center every day for a month. Then, when she was offered the choice of returning to school or getting a job, she found work on her own at an ice cream parlor. The job wasn't easy. One day Lisa had to walk three miles to and from the ice cream parlor in the rain just to work a two-hour shift. But she did it, with no complaints.

But Lisa still didn't have the self-esteem to live a straight life. Within a month after starting to work, she left home to live with a friend named Judy who had dropped out of PDAP.

The two girls paid for their doping by shoplifting. When Judy got arrested, her father would always bail her out. But when Lisa got caught, Dot and Bart let her stay in the juvenile center for two full days.

"We actually forced the courts to prosecute her. It cost us two hundred fifty dollars to pay an attorney, but we felt it was better for Lisa to get a juvenile conviction than to come before the courts as an adult. And she was almost seventeen," said Dot.

Their tough love was to pay off in the end. Lisa was probated to PDAP for a year. This time she had no choice but to stay in the program. For a full month she was hostile. Then suddenly Lisa began to work the Twelve Steps. She was put on the steering committee. Again she seemed to be doing very well. Then she turned seventeen. She was very frightened to realize that under the law she could be considered an adult.

"For about six weeks she went through a crisis. We could tell she wanted to dope and fall back into her old habits," said Dot. "The game she was playing was that she would try to mess up at home so that we would get upset and tell her she was a failure. If she could have gotten us to do that, she could have gone back on the streets, leaving the counselors, Bart, and myself to take the blame. She wouldn't have to be responsible for the consequences herself."

But no one fell for this con. The counselors, Bart, and Dot just kept telling her, "Whatever you do, Lisa, it's really okay. It's your life."

All the while she was acting up at home, Lisa was serving on the steering committee, trying to set a good example for the other youngsters! Later Lisa told her parents, "Being on the steering committee forced me to be okay for part of the time, because I wanted to present a responsible image."

Gradually her actions at home began to follow her behavior at PDAP, and she began to accept the full responsibility for herself. She got a job, moved into her own apartment, and began to grow. Now she has had nine months of sobriety. She hopes to become a counselor soon. Her parents believe she will reach her goal.

"Lisa has learned a lot about being responsible through having to support herself," said Dot. "She didn't have to get her own apartment, but she chose to do it. We give her some help, but she fully realizes we are not obligated to do anything we don't want to. When she asks for something we don't feel she should have, we turn her down. We are very proud of Lisa. At last she is really making it."

One reason Lisa has succeeded, Dot believes, is that she and Bart have remained in PDAP. They didn't give up.

"If you stick with the program and believe in it, if you do what the program tells you to, I really believe that your drug abuser will come around," she now tells newcomers to PDAP.

Both Bart and Dot believe PDAP has benefited them in their careers, too. Bart has stopped trying to control his co-workers. Dot has learned to say, "I'm not willing," rather than arguing with the employees she manages. All three found a different conception of their Higher Power. Bart said, "I realized there was some higher being who created the universe, but I didn't have much contact. When PDAP-ers told me to turn over the well-being of a daughter on the streets to this Higher Power, I just couldn't do it. I didn't really believe that God could take away the things that I knew were making my life unmanageable either.

"So, I read a lot of books by Jess Lair and Og Mandino. I studied transactional analysis. Finally I realized there really was a Higher Power greater than myself. I would just walk around repeating the Serenity Prayer, and finally I got to where I could tell my Higher Power that I was turning Lisa over to him . . . that I had absolutely no control over her . . . that Lisa had her life in her own hands with whatever help he could give her."

Dot said, "I always felt that God was inside me, but now I know that for many years I didn't listen to him. I suppressed my Higher Power. By exercising my self-will, I took away his power to help me.

"The last time Lisa was on the streets, another parent said, 'If there is a Higher Power, why isn't he doing something about Lisa?' And I explained that God could only do for Lisa what she allowed him to do, just as had been true in my own life. When we're willing to listen to him, that's when he takes over in our lives."

Lisa said, "My Higher Power is the group. When I have close relationships with others, I know that my contact with the Higher Power is good. I can pray for awareness and get it, but I usually get it by hearing the answers from the other people in the group."

Dot, Bart, and Lisa all recognize that their lives are not problem-free. But through working the Twelve Steps, they know that they can have a very beautiful family relationship.

Chapter Five

The Family That Didn't Have to Suffer

Of Ted and Hazel's three sons, Colin had been the most difficult to raise. The two older boys had always made their parents proud. They had won medals in music. They had made good grades. But Colin had been so hyperactive that he had not been able to sit still long enough even to practice on the drums.

Long ago a doctor had prescribed daily medication for his hyperactivity and the school had placed him in special education classes. His reading did not improve. Almost friendless, he seemed to specialize in making life miserable for everyone, including his family.

Until the boy became an adolescent, Ted felt he could communicate well with his son. Then Colin began to "clam up." He didn't want to be touched. When Ted tried to rumple his hair or pat him on the shoulder, Colin pushed away.

Knowledgeable about drugs because of his profession, Ted recognized that Colin was in trouble with mind-changing chemicals long before Hazel did. When he was almost seventeen, the boy started reading Ted's professional magazines avidly.

"How nice," Hazel commented to Ted. "Maybe he'll want to follow in your footsteps."

"No, I don't think so," Ted said. "And I don't want him reading my magazines—period." He knew that drugs prescribed for the family often disappeared and liquor from his cabinet seemed to evaporate. He also knew that at times Colin was stoned. But he never told Hazel. He hoped the situation would not get worse.

Ted often heard Colin bragging on the phone to a friend, "Boy, I sure got stoned on that drug," and naming a pill about which he had read. Ted figured that Colin was craving friends. He could get stoned—or act like it or even talk about taking pills—and find a group of dopers who would accept him.

"It was as if Colin was saying, 'I can't play a musical instrument and I can't be a genius, but I can get stoned better than anyone,'" Ted said.

All that summer, when Colin lay around in bed refusing to look for a summer job, Hazel never suspected drugs. "I thought Colin couldn't get into trouble like that if he didn't have a car," she said.

The reason Ted didn't tell Hazel was that he didn't feel he could do anything about Colin's doping. He and Hazel both worked. They couldn't sit around the house babysitting a seventeen-year-old twenty-four hours a day. He figured that Colin would refuse to go to a psychiatrist. So, why worry Hazel? Maybe Colin would grow out of this phase of his life.

Eventually Colin did get a job, but he began to spend all his paycheck on pot, dope, and pills. All the other kids who worked with him were on drugs, too. Finally Ted confronted Colin in front of Hazel.

"Sure, I'm smoking pot. So what? Everybody I know smokes pot," he said. Ted and Hazel didn't like what Colin was doing, but they didn't see how they could make him stop.

"Okay," they said, "we know we can't keep you from smoking pot. But we don't want you to get arrested. Smoke it in the house if you have to, but whatever you do, don't go sneaking around outside doing it."

One day Ted caught his tall, skinny teen-ager escorting some rough-looking girls into his bedroom and closing the door. He believed that Colin was trading pot for sex. Something had to be done, so he told Colin he had to go to a Family Service psychologist. Colin became abusive, but Ted insisted.

"But I won't talk," Colin warned. "You can't make me.".

First the psychologist talked to Ted and asked if he approved of Colin's doping.

"No," said Ted.

"Then why do you let him do it?"

So Ted told Colin he couldn't use marijuana in the house anymore. Nor could he close the door to his room or have his weird friends in. The result was that he soon caught Colin smoking a hookah in the backyard.

After a few sessions, the psychologist admitted that he

was getting nowhere with Colin. He suggested Ted take him to a PDAP center at a nearby church.

"Oh, no, not a church!" said Ted. He was Jewish and he didn't want to get involved with any Christian group. But the psychologist assured him PDAP was nonsectarian. Ted made the appointment.

As Ted and Hazel sat outside the counselor's office while Colin was being interviewed, they heard him yelling.

"Then the counselor came out and told us that Colin had no intention to work the program," said Ted. "We had to tell Colin he had the choice of either getting into PDAP or leaving home before he agreed to go to PDAP's night meetings for thirty days."

They dropped a very angry Colin off at his first PDAP meeting—but picked up a grinning one. He was with two ratty-looking boys.

"These guys want me to go have coffee with them," said Colin. Ted noticed that the kids looked just like his doping buddies.

"Look, we got you in this program to get you straight. You're not fooling us. You're going to go out and get high, aren't you?"

"No, Dad, that's not the way it is," Colin said. "You wanted me in PDAP. Now let me go. They'll bring me home."

Against his better judgment, Ted gave permission. He was amazed when Colin did come home absolutely sober.

After the second meeting, Colin asked to go to an all-night party afterward.

"We thought, oh boy, here he goes again with the

dope, the cars, the whole bit," said Hazel. But again he came home sober.

The third meeting was on a Saturday morning when Hazel was at home. She was surprised when a big bunch of PDAP-ers came into the house with Colin after the meeting. She could hear them making a lot of rustling and rattling noises in his room. Finally Colin came out with a suitcase in his hand.

"These kids think I should move out and go live with some PDAP-ers for thirty days. See, they have a car, and they can take me to the day center every day," said Colin.

Hazel looked at the son who had presented her with so many nerve-racking crises. "Sure," she said.

"I guess I was relieved to have Colin go. I was tired of all the hassle of having a drug abuser at home. Maybe it was selfish of me, but at the time I just wanted him out of my sight," she said.

After they left, she went into his room. The wastebasket was crammed with all Colin's marijuana paraphernalia. The PDAP-ers had broken up his big pipe and cleaned out all his marijuana papers. She was so happy she could have cried. Ted was glad, too.

They didn't realize that it would be months before they saw Colin again. During that time he did not even phone to ask for money or a car.

Didn't their son care about them at all? Ted and Hazel wondered. They started going to the PDAP parent meetings, hoping they would catch a glimpse of Colin as he went to the young people's meeting which was held in the same church.

"Colin never came upstairs to the parent meetings as

some of the kids did. We got the impression that he really didn't want to see us, and we didn't like it. But the counselor told us, 'Leave him alone. Just stay off his back for awhile. He's straight and working the program. You'll get back together, but it's going to take time.'"

So for six long months they didn't try to make contact. In fact, for most of that time they didn't even know where he was living. Once when Hazel saw Colin coming out of the young people's meeting, she started to go up to him, but Colin turned away. That hurt! Hazel started to cry, and one of the PDAP girls came and put her arms around her.

One thing gave them comfort. If they missed a parent meeting, other PDAP-ers would say, "Hey, I saw Colin and he wanted to know why you weren't at the meeting last time." Even though Colin did not want to be with them, he did want to be reassured that they were all right.

After four months, Ted and Hazel went to a Round Robin and saw Colin with a bunch of PDAP-ers.

"He looked so happy he was glowing," said Hazel. "It was like PDAP was what he had been looking for his whole life. He came up to me and said, 'I heard you felt that I didn't want to see you.' That's the best he could say.

"At the time I still didn't know the program well enough to keep my serenity. I was hurting. But I had to admit that Colin was doing very well in taking the responsibility for his own life. If he could do that better without me than with me, I knew that letting go of him had to be the first priority.

"After about six months, Colin started coming to the

house again. But after only about a half hour with us he became very edgy. He would start acting hyper again and have to get out rapidly.

"Even so, we were so happy to see him the first couple of times that we would have done anything he asked. And he and I fell into a ridiculous relationship. The counselor had said that as long as Colin was living with PDAP-ers and staying chemically free and doing everything right, then it was okay for us to pad his corners with a little financial help. That was all it took for me to start playing a very bad game. When Colin asked me for money, I gave it to him, no questions asked. He knew it was better for him if he didn't take it. But I was such an easy mark that he just kept on following past patterns.

"All the while," said Hazel, "I knew that Colin was being careless with money. Once I saw two of his paychecks lying loose on the front seat of his car. They could easily have gotten lost! I really was burned up about that, but I kept right on giving him money."

One night Colin called when his mother had the flu.

"Mom, I locked myself out of the apartment and had to kick the door down. Now the manager says I have to pay a hundred dollars for the damage," he said. Hazel felt as if her head would burst wide open.

"Well, you can just pay for it yourself. I don't want to hear any more about money," she snapped. That was the end of the "Gimme" game. Since that day Colin has never asked for a cent—except as a joke.

Ted and Hazel went regularly to parent meetings during the months when Colin was avoiding them.

"I wish I could say that we worked the Steps all the

way through, but we did not. Perhaps it was because we didn't have to suffer the pain with Colin that a lot of PDAP parents did with their drug abusers. Colin never went to jail. We didn't have to put him out of the house. Colin liked PDAP right away. And he got straight right away," said Hazel.

"Even so, PDAP helped me gain insight into myself. I've been able to accept myself completely for the first time. I see that I'm not the only one who is 'dented.' Everybody has faults and it's really okay.

"I used to be such a perfectionist that when I drove up to a stop light, I even worried about what the person in the next car was thinking about me. I used to back off from other people because I was afraid they would hurt me. Now I love talking to everyone.

"I once thought money was important. Now I realize that big houses and expensive cars don't mean anything if you can't hack it inside yourself. In PDAP I learned that the greatest thing in life is being able to talk freely, knowing that what I say will be accepted—even if I tell about fouling up."

Ted did get a sponsor and wrote his inventory, but he has not worked any further Steps. He felt that he came into PDAP with a lot of insights that others learn in the program. He liked the confrontations he got from other parents, counselors, and his sponsors, however. They gave him a chance to grow some more.

When Colin started visiting his parents, Ted knew the program well enough to recognize that it was good for Colin to express his anger openly.

"Once I told him I thought he needed a mechanic to fix his car. Colin yelled back, 'Dad, you make me mad as

----! I want to kick your ---- in.' I was delighted to hear him communicating his feelings like that. Before PDAP, he would never have had the courage to say it," said Ted.

About ten months after Colin joined PDAP, he made his amends to his dad. One day he brought a friend with him to the house. For the first time Colin admitted to his dad that he used to steal his liquor and do a lot of other things that neither of them had ever discussed. Colin apologized and Ted easily forgave him.

Colin quickly changed from a young man who didn't want to touch or communicate to one who could tell both his parents, "I love you," and hug and kiss them.

About a year after Colin became a PDAP-er, Ted and Hazel went to the PDAP annual banquet. There they saw a sight they could never have imagined. Colin, dressed in a white tuxedo with tails, was escorting a pretty PDAP girl in a pink formal! Colin looked so ridiculous they wanted to laugh. He looked so happy and clean that they wanted to cry. They felt themselves beaming with an unfamiliar response—pride for the son that had been so difficult to raise.

For two and a half years Colin has continued to progress.

"Sometimes we wish he could go faster. He wasn't invited to be on the steering committee for a full year. But then, Colin wasn't like some of the kids who really had to bottom out. He never got arrested. He never overdosed. But, he's never had a slip that we know of, either. He graduated from high school by getting his G.E.D. and he has even taken one college course," said Ted.

Ever since he stopped asking for money, Colin has supported himself through a succession of jobs. He shares an apartment with two other rent-paying PDAP-ers and a perennial bunch of new PDAP-ers who don't have jobs. His mother worries about his "gypsy existence," but keeps her serenity and counts her blessings.

At nineteen Colin is calmer—without any medication—than ever before. He has stopped smoking and started gaining needed weight. He seems more self-controlled and self-assured. He is totally involved in PDAP—and wants to be a counselor some day.

The Mother
Who Never
Made Waves_____

When Eva and Bill first noticed irrational behavior in their teen-agers, they did not believe that chemicals were at fault. Eva tells what happened in her own words.

_____

Bill and I first started hearing the word *marijuana* when our son, Jim, was thirteen. It was about the same time that he and his sister, Susie, who was fourteen and a half, began wearing blue jeans, looking dirty, and letting their unwashed, uncombed hair grow long. Their grades dropped right off their report cards.

Jim and Susie admitted they had tried pot. They talked to us freely about it. We weren't too concerned about a drug problem. We worried more about their poor schoolwork and sloppy appearance.

"Our kids are really not into drugs," we told each

other. "Smoking pot is just part of the times, just a teen-age phase." Then as an afterthought, one or the other of us would sigh and say, "Oh, God, how nice it will be when they get back to normal!"

All we said to Jim and Susie was, "Don't smoke that pot in the house. It's illegal."

We weren't aware that we were denying the very root of their problems, but we were. Over the years we continued this deliberate blindfolding of our eyes until Jim's doping became so bad that we thought he needed to be committed to a mental hospital forever. We did not see clearly that drugs were the problem until five wretched years later.

Our denial stemmed from the fact that nothing in our lives had prepared us for what it meant to have a doper in our family. Bill and I had always been successful. Early in our marriage we started a small business, and I worked as a full partner. The company grew nationwide. The money just seemed to roll in. We lived in a big house, sent our four children to the best private schools, and gave them all the material possessions they could desire.

We thought our family relations were super, too. I tried very hard to make all the children realize Bill and I loved them, because I felt that love had not been openly expressed to me while I was growing up. As the mother, I was responsible for "making" everyone happy. I didn't want to be a controlling parent with a lot of rules. My philosophy of mothering was, "Don't make waves." During their preadolescence, the children never got into trouble.

When Jim started making bad grades, he complained

that private school was too demanding. We allowed him to attend the public junior high for the eighth grade. Soon Jim was bringing home friends who looked even grubbier than his old ones. He flunked the eighth grade.

Then Jim and Susie started climbing out the window late at night to drive our car. We lectured them, but gradually came to accept their staying out till almost any hour as normal. Again our denial of the facts kept us from taking a stand. We did not realize that serious drug problems grow by midget steps.

By the time Jim painted his room red and purple and installed black lights and rock star posters, I had accepted hippy ways as being typical for all teen-agers. Even when the smell of incense kept floating down the stairs, I never confronted him. I told myself that the children's bedrooms were their own private domain. I wanted him to be happy and have friends, didn't I? He wasn't making any waves, was he? Besides, marijuana was not a problem.

But I was angry when Jim received another handful of Fs. I just didn't think I could take his refusal to study any longer. Jim needed to develop self-discipline and I was going to see that he did it. I painted a big poster that read, "Shape up or ship out," and thumbtacked it to his purple wall. That night Bill and I told him, "Whatever you become is up to you."

The words we said were right. I wasn't going to nag anymore. But inside, emotionally, I was holding on to his failure as tightly as ever. I would still feel my gut twisting and gnawing. My anxiety caused me to act in ways that I now realize were insane.

One morning I got so angry when Bill couldn't wake

Jim and the kids were late for school that I turned my car right into the path of another on the freeway. I totalled the station wagon and was lucky to get by with some cracked ribs. I blamed my carelessness on the fact that Bill was too passive!

When Jim was sixteen, we let him attend a private boarding school in Colorado. At the end of the year, Jim's report card showed all Bs. Bill and I were so pleased that we rewarded Jim with his first car. He immediately took off in it to visit a friend in California. In fact, he spent the whole summer traveling around the country, existing mostly on the money we sent him.

Now I know that Jim's doping had been very minor while he was at the private school in Colorado. But that summer he learned almost everything there was to know about hard drugs. And we made it easy for him by padding his corners with the car and the money. When he returned to the Colorado school in the fall, he didn't stay long. In October we received a strange phone call from him.

"I'm writing a book and the teachers won't let me work on it. I've just got to finish it. Please let me come home," he said. We refused, but Jim came home anyway.

Jim's book was all very philosophical with a lot of God-talk in it. I thought it a strange mixture of Christianity and Buddhism, the kind heard about so much in the seventies. Jim's grandmother read it and thought he was called to the ministry. But I felt a cold shiver of real fear. What was going on in my son's head?

Now that I know more about drugs, I realize that dopers may truly feel very spiritual. Hard drugs can cause the mind to feel as if it is in touch with God. And Jim was now doping with something considerably harder than pot.

Once Jim was at home, he stopped writing. He spent his days lying around the house sleeping and his nights roaming around in his car. On our insistence, Jim spent a few weeks going to school. Then he dropped out. After a few more weeks of nagging from us, he got a job, which he soon quit. Then the cycle repeated itself.

Every day Jim's empty eyes and vacant face made him look a little more weird. A chilling thought came to us. Could our son be mentally ill? I was really worried.

By this time I was separated from my husband and in the process of ending my marriage. I was depressed about the pending divorce and gloomy about Jim's psychotic appearance.

I would not have admitted it at the time, but I was so immersed in my own pain that I just wanted the situation with him to go away. I felt like telling him, "Don't mess with my life."

The way I lived was truly insane. Susie was at college, my younger son was living with his dad. My thirteen-year-old daughter and I contained ourselves in one part of the house while Jim moved to a room that had its own entrance. He came and went as he pleased. We ate at different times and seldom saw each other.

Even though Bill and I were separated, he still wanted to help Jim. But every time we talked on the phone about him was pure agony to me. The only way to make some of the inner pain go away was to take a good, stiff drink every night.

Soon I was forced to admit that something had to be

done about Jim. He didn't *do* strange things. He just *seemed* very strange. It was almost as if he were in a catatonic state—a body with a mind existing in another world. At last I took him to a psychiatrist who said he needed to be hospitalized.

Jim didn't argue. Since he was eighteen by now, he signed himself into the locked mental ward of a general hospital for fourteen days, the minimum stay. At the end of this period, the psychiatrist said that Jim was still extremely disoriented. He needed extended care.

Did the psychiatrist mean that Jim was psychotic? Bill and I just couldn't believe he was in such bad shape. We told ourselves that Jim looked much better and let him come home. But within three months he was almost catatonic again. He committed himself to a different hospital for fourteen days, but again insisted on coming home after the minimum stay. The psychiatrist prescribed medication that was supposed to allow him to function on the outside.

At the time I was relieved that Jim was taking an antipsychotic pill. Now I realize that this kind of medication was exactly what a drug addict like Jim didn't need. The psychiatrist simply had substituted a prescription drug for all the illegal ones Jim had been swallowing. He wasn't one bit better off!

The crisis came when Jim landed in jail. He had been spinning his car around on an empty parking lot when a policeman stopped him and searched his car. The officer found nothing. But Jim later told Bill, "There was so much love in that policeman's eyes that I just pulled out the thirty pills I had and handed them to him." Jim must have been really freaked out to have done that!

Since we retained the best attorney in town, Jim received only a two-year probated sentence, a much lighter penalty than was usual. But if I had been anxious before, I was now a nervous wreck. Jim was still doping. Even when I warned him that he would go straight to prison if he were caught with drugs only once, he kept right on.

Prison was one of the only three alternatives I believed possible for Jim at that time. The other two were that he would "O.D." (overdose) or that he would commit suicide. I began spending my evenings drinking, watching TV, and waiting for Jim to come home. The alcohol relaxed me and helped me forget my worries about him and the pain of divorce.

Gradually I started taking my first drink earlier in the day. Eventually I came to be never really drunk, but never really sober, either. At the time I didn't think about the fact that my alcoholic patterns were just as sick as Jim's doping habits. I, too, was using a chemical escape hatch without realizing it.

By this time Jim was using a lot of acid, a lot of mushrooms. One night when my daughter had a girl friend spending the night, he knocked on her door at 1:30 A.M. She found Jim on his knees, ranting about Jesus and God, completely out of his mind. He didn't attempt to hurt her, but she was so terrified that she asked for a lock on her bedroom door. I put one on mine, too. Night after night I lay behind the locked door, longing for sleep to blot out the pain I felt.

It seemed to me that I was watching Jim disintegrate physically and mentally. He was underweight and sickly. He never associated with friends anymore. He just walked the streets alone at night, came home, and slept till about three the next afternoon. During the day I never checked to see if he was in bed. I was afraid I would find him dead.

Now Bill and I began to believe that the psychiatrist had been right. Jim *was* psychotic. He needed extended care. I began to make inquiries at the Menninger Foundation, the best psychiatric hospital I knew of.

About the same time, my own emotional pain and drinking caused me to go to Alcoholics Anonymous, where I heard about PDAP. I made an appointment with the PDAP counselor and began pouring out all my misery to him.

"But you don't have to live that way," he said. He wasn't blaming me. He just seemed concerned.

"What do I have to do?"

"Just turn it all over to God. Let go," he said.

"But I have let go," I said and told him how I had made Jim responsible for his own grades long ago.

"I'll bet you're the kind of mother who fixes breakfast for your son every morning—and does everything else for him, too," he said. I laughed because he had described me exactly.

"We're going to ask you to make a 180 degree turnabout in your ideas about what a good mother should do. Just let go. Don't worry about anything between today and tomorrow. Get him in to see me, any way you can."

I was surprised to find that night that I really could turn Jim and his problems over to God. I wasn't too spiritual, but I had long ago given up on the thought that I could do anything to change him. So I just prayed,

"Here, God I'm giving him to you. He's out of my hands." Then I actually went to sleep.

The next day I told Jim I had met some neat people in a drug abuse program. I thought he might enjoy meeting them, too. Jim didn't protest too much. But after he had talked with the counselor and watched some of the teen-agers in the day center, he said, "Boy, would I like to get some of those kids high. We could really have a good time."

It was clear that Jim wasn't interested in PDAP, but I was. I went to the parent meetings, and began to feel better. "Work on the Twelve Steps with your own improvement rather than Jim's in mind," my sponsor told me. "All you can do for him is to accept him as he is, love him, and let him bottom out."

The love of the other parents who had been through similar experiences helped me begin to make that 180 degree turn that the counselor had mentioned. One morning when I was driving Jim to the psychiatrist, I noticed his eyes were bloodshot—a sure sign he had been smoking pot. But I said nothing.

"Mom, you act like it's not bothering you any more when I'm high," Jim finally said. I smiled.

"Jim, it's not," I said. I had completely released him. I had achieved serenity, even as Jim continued to deteriorate.

Finally one night Jim came into the room where I was reading. His face was contorted with pain.

"Jim, you're hurting," I said. He looked as if he would cry.

"Yes, Mom, I am. I've just screwed up my life so bad! And I don't know what to do."

"Would you like to talk to the PDAP counselor?" I asked. And he said yes!

The counselor advised Jim to go to the hospital. We learned that the hospitals that work with PDAP aim at total sobriety rather than substituting a prescribed drug for an illegal one.

Once again Jim committed himself. This time he stayed thirty days. When he came home, he seemed healthy. His eyes were clearer. He appeared normal again.

I spent some time walking on eggshells, because I had been told that Jim couldn't stand any kind of pushing. The PDAP parent meetings helped me understand how to continue to let go. Even when Jim slipped and drank four bottles of beer out of a six-pack I had bought for a visiting friend, I kept my serenity. I walked right past him and the empties without saying a word. In a few minutes he came to me.

"Mom, I want to apologize to you for drinking beer," he said.

"Jim, I can't control that. You don't ever need to apologize to me for drinking. I won't take the responsibility for your slipping or not slipping, but if I had known that beer in the house was a threat to your sobriety, I wouldn't have brought it in. I'll go and pour out the rest."

Jim just grinned. "I thought you weren't going to take on my responsibility," he said. "I'll go pour it out myself."

Later Jim told me that even after his thirty days in the hospital it took him another three months to make a genuine commitment to go straight. In a way he wanted to be sober, but he hadn't made the gut decision to be that way.

Once he developed a lot of friendships in PDAP, however, he did get completely straight. After three years, he is twenty-one years old and still involved with the program. A year ago he got a high school diploma through PDAP's G.E.D. school. Now he has his own apartment and tries to support himself completely (though his father sometimes rescues him with a check when he is between jobs).

However, I have had to accept the fact that emotionally Jim is only sixteen. He was so high almost all the time between the ages of thirteen and eighteen that he missed out on five years of learning how to relate to others. He still gets tickets for driving too fast. He dates girls much younger than he. He switches jobs frequently with no thought about what his eventual career should be.

But I have seen a lot of progress. Right after Jim joined PDAP he moved into an apartment with three other PDAP-ers. Clothes and garbage littered the rooms. These young men who had just broken out of the chrysalis of drug addiction could not yet believe they had beautiful wings with which to fly. They were still in the caterpillar stage, grubbing around in the dirt.

Now Jim lives in his own apartment. It looks calm and warm—not spick and span—but very nice. It's the home of someone who clearly respects himself. Often he invites new PDAP-ers to live with him.

As for our family, we have all changed for the better, too. Jim's older sister is now married. Susie has told me she stopped using marijuana while in high school because she recognized it made her depressed. The younger children do not want anything to do with drugs, not even pot, though they do take an occasional drink. They tell me they just don't want to go through all the pain that Jim went through.

Bill has remarried, but he is still very much involved in helping me raise the children. He does not go to PDAP parent meetings, but through my actions has learned somewhat to let go.

As for myself, working the Twelve-Step program has made a wonderful difference. In doing my inventory I discovered many surprising things. Even though I had always presented to the world the image of the perfect mother, the perfect wife, and the perfect career woman, I felt anything but perfect. Inside I lived with a lot of fear and anxiety. I felt so bad about myself I became an overachiever.

I went to college, got two degrees, married a man I loved very much, had four beautiful children, and developed a satisfying career.

I was a pleaser. If others weren't happy, I took on their unhappiness myself. Whenever my husband had emotional aches and pains, I, too, carried them in my gut. The result was that I gave him the power to make me feel inferior. By taking on his anxieties, I got hooked into not feeling good about myself. And then I resented him.

Many friends wonder how I have been able to maintain such friendly relations with my ex-husband. The Twelve Steps taught me to recognize that I was powerless over his feelings. When he became anxious over what the children were doing, I learned to let his anxiety go and remain peaceful. He was miserable, but I didn't have to let myself get hooked into feeling responsible for solving his misery. I could "change the things I can"—myself.

I began to relate to my chilren differently, too. In the past, I trained them to talk through me to their father. And I carried his reply back to them. This strange game evolved because I always tried to shield the children from their father's abruptness.

Today I realize that I was wrong when I felt that I knew how to love the children better than Bill did. Sure, I was tender, sharing, and gentle; their father didn't know how to show emotions or express feelings. The way he demonstrated his love was by buying them a new car or anything else he could buy. I used to resent this emphasis on material things, but today I realize that I don't love my children any better. His love for them is just as deep as mine, but he expresses it differently. When I stopped being the go-between, the children developed healthy relationships with him.

Even more astounding to me is the fact that by releasing my children and loving myself more and making it okay for me to be just the person I am, the children have become closer to me.

Now I no longer require myself to be perfect. I realize that I can sit down and do nothing. I can watch soap operas or spend an entire day reading a book—and it's really all right for me to do it. I used to be ruled by productivity. I thought I had to make more money or run the house better than anyone else. Now I have inner goals. I know I can achieve just by being the person I am meant to be.

Sharing my inventory with another person brought me a wonderful feeling of humility and a oneness with God. After I had done it, I could accept both the positive and negative about myself. I could see that, yes, I was different—as is everyone else. But basically we are all one.

What working a Twelve-Step program does for me is to keep me from having anxiety. It keeps me in the positive, in the spiritual, in the freedom. It keeps me sane. I cannot exist in the way I want to exist without it.

And as for my Jim, I am convinced that the Twelve Steps and PDAP saved his life.

Chapter Seven

The Mother Who Learned From Pain

Like many single parents, Monica feared she had made lots of mistakes in rearing her children. When they became drug abusers, she punished herself. Here is how Monica describes the changes that PDAP made in her children's lives and in her own.

Sometimes people look at me strangely when I tell them that if I had the opportunity to change my past life I wouldn't do it. After all, it was pure misery going through two divorces and being faced with the fact that two of my three children had drug habits. It was painful trying so hard to make me and the kids look perfect so we could present to the world an image that wasn't as bad as I feared it was.

Because of all that misery, however, I found PDAP.

Now I work a Twelve-Step program. I have a happy marriage and three children who have learned to take the responsibility for their own lives. We all know how to share our feelings, both bad and good ones. We can let ourselves be vulnerable so that we may love other people rather than fear them. For the first time in my life, I know how to live!

My story really begins with the faulty decision I made as a child. Somehow I thought I was bad and everyone else was good. I learned to put on a good front. I covered up that feeling very well.

At twenty, I was expecting my first child, living away from my parents for the first time, and feeling extremely homesick. Even before Kevin was born, I knew that my marriage was a disaster. I was hurting, but suddenly I had a tiny baby who had needs of his own. I didn't want to hold him or love him.

Only fourteen and a half months later I gave birth to Stan. My unhappiness caused me to cling to the younger baby. I couldn't hold him enough. I really loved him.

Meanwhile, Kevin had become a curious little toddler, who constantly was messing up the apartment which I tried to keep spotless. Sometimes he would run outside when I wasn't watching him. When Kevin did that, I would be so angry that I would hit him with a belt until he had big black and blue marks on his legs, back, and buttocks. More than once I banged his head on the floor.

Though I often felt guilty after I punished him so severely, I did not realize at the time that I was a child abuser. Now I know that I saw Kevin's misbehavior, as I called his normal toddler activities, as proof of my failure as a parent. I just had to try to control him so that no one would know how badly I felt about myself.

Cynthia was born five years after Stan. Soon I had two failed marriages, but I was determined that the children would put on a good front for the world to see. When the boys brought home Bs and Cs on their report cards, I would tell them, "You can do better than that." Nothing less than an A would do.

I always made sure my house was shiny clean. I worked hard at my career and became financially successful. From the outside we looked as presentable as last year's gaily decorated Easter eggs. Inside I felt as rotten. I lived with a great deal of fear and guilt.

When Kevin was about fifteen and we were living in Indiana, he came home one night acting so strangely I could tell he was under the influence of some kind of drug. I have never been much of a drinker myself. I don't keep alcohol and I don't like taking pills, so I was really scared. I took him to the nearest emergency room and learned he'd been smoking marijuana.

"It's not addictive," said the doctor. "You don't have to worry."

I was relieved. I gave Kevin a good lecture and let him go at that. But then he began skipping classes at school and making poor grades. I tried bribing him to do better schoolwork, but he became more hostile by the day. So I asked the school psychologist to test him.

"This boy is a very normal, curious kid. There's nothing really out of the ordinary about him," he told me. I sighed. If there was nothing wrong with Kevin, then obviously something was wrong with me, or Kevin would make better grades.

I decided I wasn't being strict enough. I started grounding Kevin when he cut classes. Soon he was slipping out his bedroom window whenever he pleased. I withheld allowances. I screamed at him. I cried. Kevin didn't change.

A move to Florida and then to Texas didn't help. We'd been in Texas only two weeks when the police picked Kevin up for shoplifting. My son was getting into real trouble, but what was I to do? I was working. I couldn't watch my kids all the time.

Two months later the assistant principal of the junior high—not Kevin's high school—called me.

"We have caught Kevin on our playground with marijuana," he said. "We want you to come down to the police station for a conference."

I was as furious at Kevin as I used to be when he was a toddler. All the way to the police station I alternately raged at Kevin and blamed myself. "After all, Kevin comes from a broken home," I told myself.

Kevin's principal expelled my son for forty-five days, but said that he could return to school within thirty days if he would join PDAP. Kevin and I both made thirty-day commitments to PDAP in a hurry.

I got a pleasant surprise at my first parent meeting. Nobody blamed me for Kevin's using marijuana. When I started apologizing for the fact that Kevin came from a broken home, another mother said to me, "Do you really love your children?"

"Yes, but . . ." I said.

"Then remember that you did the best job you possibly could. You gave them all the love you had to give them in the only way you knew how to give it at the time."

"But . . ."

"And another thing. You didn't put that first marijuana cigarette in Kevin's mouth. He made the choice, not you. In fact, you tried to persuade him not to smoke it."

What a load of guilt dropped off my shoulders! I *had* always loved my children and wanted the best for them. I really *had* tried very hard to keep Kevin from becoming a doper. Perhaps I wasn't such a failure as a mother after all.

I began to work PDAP's Twelve Steps very hard. I quickly learned acceptance. I would remind myself that I was powerless to stop my children from doping or smoking cigarettes or making bad grades.

Meetings on tough love made me realize that I had been wrong bribing Kevin to make good grades, scolding and grounding him. I learned that when parents don't try to rescue them, kids learn through their painful experiences to take responsibility for their own grades and behavior.

Kevin got his monkey's fist without a hitch, though I learned later that he really had not been chemical-free throughout that month. He accepted the fist under false pretenses.

When Kevin returned to school he and a friend named Casey got high. I was heartsick. I talked to other PDAP parents and decided what I had to do.

I told Kevin, "I'm going to give you a choice, and I'm doing it because I love you. Either be drug free or get out of the house." I didn't expect Kevin to choose to go, but he did. This experience wasn't nearly as bad as I had expected it to be, because I had a lot of support from other PDAP parents. Besides, Kevin simply moved into Casey's apartment nearby. Kevin phoned Stan and Cynthia often, so I knew he was all right. Then one day he phoned me and asked to come home.

"Not until you talk to the PDAP counselor," I said. Right away Kevin and Casey both went to the PDAP center. Since Casey's parents weren't willing to go to PDAP, the counselor asked if Casey could stay with us for awhile. He thought I would be a good influence.

Only four nights later I awoke in the middle of the night to the earsplitting sounds of the stereo. I ran into the living room and found Kevin and Casey completely spaced out.

"They've cracked the windows! They're trying to get me!" Casey yelled, cowering on the floor. "Stop them! Stop them! They've got steel bars!" Casey was a big boy, and he looked so absolutely wild that I panicked and ran for the closet. There I hid, praying for morning to come. About 6:30 I phoned Casey's father and told him something had to be done. He took both the boys to the PDAP center that morning and left them.

Later the counselor told me that the boys had been on LSD. He was referring Casey to the hospital, but he thought that Kevin could get straight by coming to the day center for another month. Kevin agreed to make the commitment, but that night he was angry at me.

"You told them I was insane," he said.

"I didn't, Kevin, but it's true," I snapped back. "Anyone who could do what you did last night has got to be insane." Kevin seemed a little scared when he heard me say that. He buckled down and worked the program for about two weeks. Then one night he came home drunk. That did it. The counselor decided that Kevin needed to go to the hospital.

He spent fourteen long weeks at the hospital. During that time I discovered that Kevin had been on pot since he was twelve. He had been on speed, too, and I had never known it.

I decided that I should get my second son, Stan, into PDAP as a preventive measure. Stan didn't have the behavior problems that Kevin had, but I was beginning to see that PDAP had a lot to offer even non-dopers. When I invited Stan to go, he said, "I don't want to be with that bunch of dopers. I don't even like those kids."

But the only chance Stan had to see Kevin now was when the hospital bussed Kevin to the regular PDAP meetings. So Stan went, just to see Kevin. And he liked PDAP right away.

After Stan began working the program for himself, he told me that he, too, had messed around with marijuana, though not as much as Kevin. He is now the strongest PDAP-er in the family.

While Kevin was in the hospital I worked on my own inventory and really faced the fact that I had been a child abuser. I had known it for years, but I had stuffed back my fears about it. I told myself, "Maybe Kevin won't remember how I used to beat him." Trying to hide the memories from myself and from him used up a lot of psychic energy. What a relief it was finally to tell Kevin's therapist about it!

She only said, "I think you were under a great deal of

pressure at the time and didn't really know any other way to handle it."

Kevin is willing to remember very little about my abuse. I told him about it. I told him I would like to go back and change all that, but I can't.

Doing my inventory made me realize that I am truly powerless over the past, just as my parents are powerless to change the things they did wrong. I have learned to forgive my mother for her mistakes, recognizing that she did the best she could at the time she did it. I know, too, it is up to Kevin to forgive me for what I did.

After Kevin left the hospital, he became completely straight for over a year. My relationship with my sons became so open, so loving and accepting that I realized something was missing in the relationship with my daughter. Cynthia never had a drug problem, but at thirteen, she was lacking in self-esteem. Like any teen-ager, she did a lot of things to test me. I found myself trying hard not to respond in the old ways.

So I urged her to join PDAP, and she did. Since then she has learned to love herself. Now that I can let go of her and allow her to be the person she really is—and even to do some things I don't like—we have achieved a closeness we never had before.

I now realize that my actions to her used to say, "If you're good, I'm going to love you. But if you're bad, I'm not." I also know that peer pressure has a lot more influence than a mother's approval.

Once when Cynthia stayed out all night without phoning, the counselors called her in. They were a lot tougher on her than I would have been. Because the counselors are very loving people, Cynthia decided to change rather than react with hostility. Since then, she has always phoned to tell me where she is at night.

Perhaps another reason why Cynthia has become a different person is because I have changed. Kevin's therapist told me that the greatest gift we can give our children is to let them see us change. If we can make changes at our "advanced age" (don't forget they see parents as very old!), then they know they can, too.

Now I am unwilling to scream at Cynthia. Instead of putting my anger on her, I share feelings. When she does something foolish, I say, "I have some fear, and the fear is coming from what might happen to you, because I love you." She accepts my feelings because she has learned to share her own feelings in PDAP.

I share my feelings at PDAP, too. I always get a lot of positive feedback when I describe the anger and guilt I used to feel as a child abuser. It's exciting to me to hear someone say they've been feeling what I've been feeling but have been afraid to admit it.

What I've learned in PDAP has also helped me make a success of my third marriage. Without that knowledge, I probably would have had my third divorce by now.

When Ron first talked about marriage, I told him that anyone who was interested in me would have to be involved in PDAP, so he started going to parent meetings.

"I can kind of relate to the boys' problem. This old knee injury I got back in high school causes me constant pain. The doctor has me on Darvon. Once I got into trouble by taking too many." he said.

How nice that he recognized the problem and solved it, I thought. Then I found out he had a source which mailed him dozens of bottles of Darvon at a time. I knew I had to confront him.

"I'm giving you the same choice I gave the kids, and I'm doing it because I love you," I said. "Either take care of your drug problem or no marriage."

That night he went to the PDAP group for abusers who are over thirty. Ron has since replaced Darvons with a mild pill that works on the inflamation. Since working the Twelve Steps he finds the pain is really not as bad as he used to believe, so he doesn't need as much medication.

The Twelve Steps have helped me overcome the inevitable friction that comes with marriage, too. Because I share my real feelings with Ron rather than covering them up, I don't explode in anger at him.

I can say, "Ron, that really hurt me," instead of nagging, fussing, or sulking. I don't have to be responsible for whatever reaction I get from him. I just share my feelings with him and let him take it from there. It's up to him to do what he wants about what I have said. It's up to me to make myself happy.

When I do get mad at Ron, I call my sponsor and share my angry feelings with her before I explode at my husband. She looks at the situation objectively and points out where the anger is coming from. By the time we are through talking, I usually have dumped out all my resentments and self-pity. Then I can share my true feelings, which are usually fears, with Ron.

After a year and a half of sobriety in PDAP, Kevin came to me one day and announced he was leaving PDAP.

"I guess I just have to find out if getting high is as much

fun as I remember it was," he said. I almost panicked. Would he slip back into his old hostilities and self-hate? What could I do? Nothing, I reminded myself. I was powerless to stop him. I knew that the more I pushed, the more he would resist.

So Kevin left PDAP. Before long he was in jail. He had gotten high with his old buddy Casey (who had left PDAP months before). Because Casey was seventeen and Kevin eighteen, the police charged Kevin with contributing to the delinquency of a minor. "I really got ripped off," was his reaction.

Although I knew I shouldn't urge him to come back to PDAP, I did. "They could get you out of jail right away," I pointed out. Immediately Kevin clammed up. I had to remind myself of my powerlessness to change him. But I could still express my feelings.

"Kevin, you know I don't approve of your getting high. But I love you and I'll always love you," I said.

"I love you, too, Mom," he said. We left it at that. He knew I wouldn't help him get out of jail. Somehow he managed to get out himself.

While Kevin was on the streets, he sometimes called and told me how lonely he was. I would just listen, tell him I loved him, but not pressure him about anything. Stan didn't urge him to come back to PDAP, either. He knew Kevin had to make that decision for himself.

We had no guarantee that Kevin would ever want to get straight again. We had to be willing to let him kill himself with dope if he wanted to do that. But I had a lot of comfort knowing that Kevin knew he could find help at PDAP anytime he wanted it.

One day Kevin phoned the counselor and asked to

come back. He had robbed a drugstore. He was terrified that the FBI was after him.

When PDAP took him back, I learned that Kevin had been on some very dangerous drugs. I don't know why he wasn't dead.

I think Kevin will stay straight this time, because he is working the Twelve Steps very hard. Some time in the future he will have to make amends for the robbery. I just have to have faith that when he does, no one will press charges.

How have I kept my serenity through all this? I have prayed a lot. I can hardly believe that I was an agnostic when I found PDAP. At first I was afraid that someone at PDAP would shove God down my throat, but no one did.

My first belief in a Higher Power was in the ability of the group to help me. I learned to trust people, and gradually I realized that a very loving God was working through those people. Because he was a very understanding God who forgave me, I began to forgive myself.

God is really here all the time, working through other people on a minute-by-minute basis. And I believe that God is going to take care of me, my husband, and my children, no matter where we are.

Chapter Eight

The Family That Was Determined to Be Perfect

For a few years after their marriage, Bob and Emily thought they would never be able to have children. When they finally did have three boys and a girl, they were determined to be perfect parents.

"We did everything we thought a family should do. We visited both sets of grandparents frequently. We went regularly to church. We took vacations together," said Bob.

"Then, when our oldest son, Tom, was about fourteen," said Emily, "it was as if he went out of the house one day and came back a total stranger." Tom had begun to buddy with some boys who were not in his Boy Scout troop. He started skipping school, wouldn't talk to his parents, and left the house earlier and stayed out later.

Eventually the phone started ringing with complaints

about Tom from school, from other mothers, and finally, from shopkeepers who had caught Tom stealing their merchandise. Bob was having to travel a lot in those days. Feeling all the responsibility for her children's behavior, Emily panicked with each call.

"You need a drink. Just calm down," Bob advised when Emily phoned him. Emily took the drink and felt better—but only for a moment.

Emily often noticed that many families who lived in the North Dakota town where she did had children who seemed to be behaving perfectly. Why couldn't she control hers? She redoubled her efforts to make her youngsters pick up their toys, clean their rooms, go to school, and make good grades. When she succeeded, she felt she was doing her duty as a mother to raise her children to be responsible human beings. She never thought—though she learned later that it was true—that she was being overprotective.

She was determined to straighten out Tom. If he slipped off at night when he should have been studying, Emily searched for him. Tom would be so angry and resentful when she found him, that his only thought was to get revenge. Once he emptied a bottle of whiskey down the drain, then told his dad that his mother had drunk it all.

Tom's strategy worked. Before long Bob and Emily were quarreling a lot. The shouting matches ended with one of them stomping angrily out of the house or slamming a door and hiding in a bedroom.

Meanwhile, Ann, who was only twelve, started becoming "difficult." If Emily tried to lecture her, she would sit in the middle of her bed and scream. Or she would run out of the house and stay away for hours. Once she was picked up by the police for panhandling. Things went from bad to worse when a juvenile judge put Tom on probation for shoplifting. At the time, Bob and Emily didn't realize that Tom was smoking marijuana and giving it to their younger children to keep them from telling on him.

The day Tom went to court, Emily said bitterly, "What are we doing wrong?"

"You ought to know," snapped Bob. "You're the one who's around him all the time. If you weren't so lenient . ."

Bob not only blamed Emily but also blamed his job for keeping him away from home. He blamed the church for not being able to make religious training meaningful to the children. He blamed the schools for not being able to prevent their students from playing hooky.

"At the time I didn't think there was any need for a change on my part," Bob said. "I figured that if I provided the home, the food, and the money to pay all the bills, and if I tried to be a pal to the boys, I had fulfilled my responsibility."

Tom kept getting into so much trouble that finally Bob and Emily had him committed to the psychiatric ward of a general hospital. After a two-day evaluation, the psychiatrist told them, "Tom is going through typical teen-age rebellion. You can't change that, but you could help by beginning family counseling."

Thus began the first step along an endless trail of psychiatrists, family counselors, school counselors, and priests. All of these professionals tried to help. But none of them did any good.

"We were too divided then, I against Bob, the kids against us," Emily explained later.

The psychiatrist tried to get Emily to see that she was being overprotective. But she and Bob had moved every two to three years. When evening came, Emily felt she had to gather the children up like a mother hen and keep them safely in the house with her.

"If the kids got into trouble at school, I would be on the phone rescuing them. If the neighbors called about something Tom had done, I made excuses. Eventually, I was going to rescue Tom right into prison," Emily said.

Still, none of the professionals laid any of the blame on drugs. Even after Ann spent six weeks in a mental hospital, the psychiatrist maintained that her problem was teen-age rebellion. Later Bob and Emily learned that many drug abusers have an uncanny ability to con even some very alert professionals. They make up plausible stories to account for their irrational behavior.

When Bob's company decided to transfer the family to Texas, both parents were thrilled. But within a few days after the move, the oldest two children had found exactly the same kind of doper friends they had before. Tom, however, was unhappy. When he wanted to return to North Dakota and get a job, Bob and Emily let him go.

Only a few months later, Tom was charged with burglary in North Dakota. He was put on probation and returned to his parents' home. While Bob and Emily were heartsick over the whole affair, they felt this experience had sobered Tom. He seemed to be taking hold of his life. He even got a job.

But then, late one night, Tom phoned from the police

station. He and his younger brother, David, who was then about fourteen, had been picked up for doing wheelies in the empty parking lot of a discount store. The police had found firecrackers and marijuana in the car. Fortunately Tom had thrown out a big bag of pot before the police searched him.

Tom had to serve a five-day sentence in city jail. He didn't like it a bit. Much later he told his parents, "When that door clanged shut and I realized that you really couldn't rescue me this time, that was when I decided I had to change."

He came home a different person. He worked hard at his job. He seemed to be off marijuana completely. But he was a miserable young man. He went to work, came home, watched television, went to bed, and repeated the same dreary cycle the next day. He did not have a single friend.

Even so, Emily and Bob began to feel more hopeful for him than for the other children. David had become just as rebellious as his big brother had ever been. The police caught him stealing auto parts. Ann was running around with a thirty-five-year-old who didn't work. By contrast, Tom seemed on the road to recovery.

Six months later their hopes were dashed when Emily answered the door one day to find two enormous Texas Rangers who wanted Tom.

"Your son broke his probation six months ago when he served time in Texas for possession of marijuana. Now he'll have to go back and finish his sentence in North Dakota," they said.

"But he's changing. He's off drugs. He's got a job," Emily protested. She called a lawyer, but he could do nothing. Tom was taken to North Dakota to serve a year's sentence.

All around him in prison, Tom saw young men smuggling drugs. They inhaled anything they could find—even spray deodorants—to get high and escape the drudgery of prison life. But Tom used his time behind bars to finish his high school education. He voluntarily took self-awareness tests. At the end of three months, he made an appeal to the judge. Since his former boss in Texas had agreed to give him back his job, he was free within four months.

Meanwhile something even more beautiful had happened in the life of this family. One Friday afternoon, Emily received a phone call from a man who said, "I have your son here with me." And the voice turned out to be not the police, or the school principal, or an irate shopkeeper, but a PDAP counselor.

Tom's stint in prison had so frightened David that he found PDAP on his own. He wanted off drugs. He wanted a different kind of life, he told the counselor. He immediately made a thirty-day commitment to PDAP. Then the counselor called Bob and Emily and asked them to make the same commitment.

By the time Tom returned from prison, the whole family was involved in PDAP. They asked Tom to go, too.

"I don't want to be involved with all those dopers," was his initial reaction. "It reminds me too much of where I've been."

"Maybe you could help someone else by sharing your experiences," Emily pointed out. But Tom let his parents know that he thought he was nothing but a loser. He hid himself in work and television programs.

Finally the family persuaded Tom to go with them to a PDAP picnic. One of the counselors invited him to look at his car. That same night, Tom became a PDAP-er, too. Soon he had lots of straight friends and fun activities. He learned to open up with his parents. From a hostile, angry young man, he changed to a serene and self-confident PDAP-er. Eventually he became a counselor.

After three years in PDAP, Bob and Emily have almost stopped trying to control their other children. Emily has quit waking Larry in the mornings. She stopped making him come home at a certain hour at night. When he got too sleepy at school, he learned to get enough sleep. She refused to nag about homework, even when his teacher asked her to "stay after him." After he flunked once, he began to study.

Bob and Emily had to practice some very tough love with Ann and David, too. They had to give Ann the choice of staying in PDAP or leaving home after she started doping again. Ann moved out and told the Child Welfare Department that her parents were abusing her two younger brothers. (The social workers inspected what Bob and Emily were doing in PDAP and quickly approved.) They kept their serenity by accepting their powerlessness to change Ann and turning her over to their Higher Power.

Now Ann is married and is gradually becoming reconciled with her parents. She told her brothers, "If Mom and Dad had padded my corners, I would still be lying around the house all day like a bum."

David has slipped and gone out on the streets more than once, too. Each time, his parents practiced acceptance, knowing that David had the PDAP tools to straighten out his life whenever he wanted to use them. And he did.

Meanwhile, Bob and Emily learned a lot about themselves by working their inventories. They used to relax by having a few beers and watching television. When the kids played the stereo too loud, Bob would "raise hell."

"After we stopped boozing all the time, we were able to work our PDAP program a lot harder. We hadn't realized how much we were into alcohol till we made a thirty-day commitment to stop using it," said Bob.

Bob and Emily no longer yell and scream at each other. When they disagree, they call their sponsors, look at the problem objectively then come back and discuss it calmly.

During the bad years, both had almost dropped out of church. Now they have a renewed faith after discovering in PDAP the necessity of being God-centered.

Emily said, "I used to think my life was like a letter—already written, stamped, and sealed. When I learned that I personally had choices, it was a revelation to me."

And Bob added, "I've found that God has sent a lot of people to help me with my problems. I'm not just a man on a raft all alone in the middle of the ocean. I can ask for help, and if I'm willing to listen and make some changes, then I know I'm not going to drown. Good things happen."

Chapter Nine

The Dope Fiend Who Got Straight

Over a period of ten years, Bill tried almost every form of mind-changing chemical available at the time. In his own words, he was a dope fiend. He was among the first addicts PDAP helped. Bill hopes his story will give parents of drug abusers insight, awareness, and hope.

I seemed to start life as a troublemaker, Bill said, when telling his story. By the time I was eight I was running with a bunch of little guys who tried to see which one could swipe the most candy and gum from the supermarket. We didn't need to steal. I was the son of a doctor. My friends' parents had plenty of money, too. We got a kick out of stealing.

By the time I was twelve, my parents figured I needed help, so they took me to a psychologist. I was hopping mad—and hurt, too. Evidently my parents considered me a little crazy because I shoplifted for fun and bullied my younger brother Fred. Yet I was no more crazy than were Mom and Dad when they screamed and yelled and fought with each other in front of us four kids. Was I any more peculiar than Mom when she wouldn't stop spanking me and Fred until we stopped crying?

No, I wasn't crazy, I told myself indignantly. I was just imitating my parents' actions. Yet I was being made to go to a psychologist while they went scot-free. I wasn't about to cooperate. I just sat and glared at the psychologist. I never told him a single thing I was thinking. So, of course, he couldn't help me.

In junior high I showed my rebellion by sneaking behind the bushes for a smoke during gym class and often skipping school. I decided that in order to be a real he-man like the tough guys in the movies, I had to drink alcohol. So one day after school, I sneaked some Scotch out of my folks' liquor cabinet and took it to a friend's house where we drank all the gin that my friend's mother had, too.

I don't remember passing out on the way home. The neighbors who found me called an ambulance. I had had such an abnormal reaction to alcohol that I was almost dead. The doctor gave me a shot of some kind of amphetamine—my first sample of speed—to revive me.

It seems that I also had an especially sensitive reaction to this chemical, too. When I came to, I was at home with Mom and Dad, chattering ninety miles an hour. To my parents, my jabbering was only a chemical with a voice. They both sat and listened to me, cracked up with laughter.

THE DOPE FIEND WHO GOT STRAIGHT

I next tried getting high by sniffing glue. A friend showed me how. It was instant joy! With a few whiffs of glue from a paper sack, I could get to a state of unconsciousness quickly, enjoy a nice high, and recover just as fast. The first time I did it, I woke up walking in circles around a pool table, cackling like a chicken. It was great!

I discovered I could do it after school and be back to normal by suppertime. My parents never knew the difference. So I sniffed glue almost every day after school for six months. But in high school, glue sniffing was considered socially unacceptable. So I began to drink again, even though alcohol was a disaster for me. Two or three beers were enough to make me sick. But they would also make me high before I passed out, and I really enjoyed the feeling of being high. It was like being crazy, being able to do anything.

Someone would say, "Hey, let's all go get crazy drunk and then we can do anything we feel like doing. We can have a good time and laugh and scream and nobody will tell us to be quiet."

So I went drunk to every high school dance and to all the football games. Getting plastered was one way of showing my rebellion to my parents because they had sent me back to a fine Catholic school rather than public school. I also fought back by sleeping through every class.

Once again my parents rescued me, by letting me go back to public school. There I found some happiness working part-time as a ranchhand for the father of my buddy, Carl. I still had visions of being a real he-man, so

I loved throwing hay, building fences, and feeding cattle.

Being an honest-to-God cowboy was so much more fun than studying that I just dropped out of school when I was sixteen. I worked for Carl's dad at five dollars a day and my room and board.

Every weekend Carl and I drove out to a little town where he had a lot of women. We had a blast getting drunk and sniffing glue and spending our entire paychecks. One day, however, I woke up in a hospital. I had sniffed so much glue that I was in intensive care.

I felt around to see if I had any broken bones. Since I didn't, I told the doctor I was ready to go back to the ranch. The doctor only smiled.

"Son, you're not going anywhere," he said. He tried to make me understand that I couldn't leave—not for thirty days. I had been committed by my parents.

As the doctor left my room, I tried to push my way past him. Two white-uniformed attendants promptly threw an arm lock on me and tossed me into a seclusion room, thus introducing me to a mental hospital. I was going to know this type of institution very well over the next decade.

Again I was angry. I played games with the psychiatrists. I broke out and holed up with a friend of Carl's. I then sent Carl to negotiate a deal with my parents. Dad told Carl to assure me that I could come home if I behaved myself. I told Dad—through Carl—that I wouldn't drink or sniff glue anymore. I would really straighten up and fly right *if* they got me transportation so that I could get a job. And Dad believed me.

THE DOPE FIEND WHO GOT STRAIGHT

My parents bought me what I wanted—a gigantic motorcycle. Since I was only five feet tall and weighed all of ninety-seven pounds, I must have looked like a gnat driving a toy. But I did get a job. I held it for six weeks before I sniffed enough glue to end up in another hospital. This time I had to stay nine months.

Once more I saw my parents' attempt to help me as a punishment. And little wonder. This hospital had all the atmosphere of a juvenile reform school. When I arrived, two boys were tying sheets together to escape through a window. We patients had riots and fights. We tatooed one another and smuggled in drugs.

A couple of junkies were the kings of our ward. The rest of us had plenty of time to watch them sit and fix. They cooked down the Darvons that somebody brought in and then shot up right in front of us. But most of us settled for downers and glue.

After another boy and I escaped for a free-wheeling weekend, the doctors were no longer willing to treat me. But my folks could see I wasn't cured. They sent me to another hospital.

There I stayed for only two weeks, but that was long enough for me to get turned on to the idea of taking hallucinogenic drugs. One of the patients was nick-named Jesus, or Mr. Love, because he had a beard, long hair, and a dreamy look. The reason he was so peaceful was that he was using mescaline, made out of peyote buttons.

One day the attendants shaved off all of Jesus' hair and zapped him with shock treatments. When he left the hospital he looked like some kind of worm, a fish. He was very straight—and very unhappy.

Somehow it seemed to me that if I were going to reach the nirvana that Mr. Peace-Love had, I needed to go out and get buzzed on LSD or some other hallucinogen. But I knew I couldn't get any acid in this hospital. I told the psychiatrist I wanted to go home and get my life together and get a job. He let me go.

What happened after this is a bit hazy to me now, because I soon was gorging myself on one kind of mind-changing chemical after another. I have no clear recollection of the events of several years.

All I know is that I was picked up by some sheriff's deputies one day and taken to a state hospital where I stayed for thirty days while Mom and Dad searched everywhere for the best private hospital in the nation for drug abusers. While they looked, I found speed. I picked the lock on the hospital drug closet, and sampled a bottle of it. I thought speed was good, but not nearly as good as the stories I'd heard about hallucinogens.

One patient had told me he used to live in Oaxaca—a beautiful Mexican spot where he lived with the Indians and ate mushrooms. Rent was only four dollars a month. All you had to do, he said, was reach up and grab a leaf off a plant and roll it up to smoke as a joint. He painted a gorgeous picture of a mellowed-out place where you could sit around high watching the rain fall. It sounded like heaven.

When Mom and Dad shipped me off to the fancy Eastern hospital, I was ready for the big time. I had heard that this hospital had STP. I planned to really do me a trip. But when I arrived, I did not find a single hallucinogen.

Right away the hospital staff found my speed and

removed it. But they didn't find the marijuana I had brought with me. I would pass out the pot in the smoking room at night so that the other patients could get high with me. One night an attendant came in. To test him, we lit up right in front of him. He didn't object. In fact, he was soon bringing us more pot. He became quite a friend. When I had a pass I often visited his house and smoked hash with him.

One day I heard that my attendant friend was in the pits because he had received his draft call. Someone told me he was out looking for some heroin to make himself feel better. I really liked this attendant. I wanted to tell him, "Hey, man, don't get on heroin. It's a drag."

I had seen junkie friends come into the hospital, kick, then go back, and promptly get addicted once more. They would tell stories about how the cops would string them between two police cars and beat on them. Everyone knew that junkies were the lowest form of human being on earth, and that the police hated them, I told the attendant. I was sure I would never get hooked on heroin.

After he left, I kept trying my hardest to get into hallucinogens. So, although the Eastern hospital had a good staff which really seemed to care about me, I did nothing but make trouble. Finally the doctors told my parents that nothing could be done for me. They kicked me out.

By now I was tired of hospitals anyway. I was almost twenty years old and still lacked a little more than a year of high school to graduate. I decided to finish my education and get a job.

During the first half of the school year, I studied hard.

I wasn't completely straight, but I didn't do dope constantly.

By the second half of the year, however, I had a chance to take some acid. Once I sampled it, I went at it in a big way. Acid never affected me visually, as so many of my friends told me it would. I didn't see walls melt, or light come out of my body, or horses jump out of pictures and gallop across the room. But acid did make me hear funny things. When people talked to me, I couldn't be sure what they were saying. When I talked back, I wasn't sure what I had said.

I loved acid. Everytime I took it, I felt like a little kid who was tickled. Everything was a joke. Acid gave me a kind of feeling "awakening." My friends and I had a lot of fun. We would go up into the attic and play with grandma's old hats. Or we would hop around the park like frogs. We would get sparklers and zap one another with them and watch the after-images.

Later on acid became horrible. I had so many bad trips that I began to carry downers with me. If a trip got too bad, I'd take a downer and just crash in order to escape the waking nightmare. By the time I quit acid, I hated it.

When I started going to junior college, I began getting into speed. I would meet my girl friend back in Houston for the weekends to get "wired." I started using the needle with her. During the week I took pills to keep me going.

When I came down with hepatitis, I used my illness as an excuse for quitting college. Then I really got into speed in a big way. I had a buddy named Sam who was part of a crazy, crazy clique I was in. Speed makes you crazy. That period between the years of twenty and twenty-two was probably the most terrifying time of my life. I watched some friends die and others go to jail.

I remember one night when Sam, three other buddies, and I sat around a table and carried on twenty-five different conversations at once. I was talking with each one of them separately, and each of them was talking to me and to all the rest at the same time.

Just about every hour, Sam would grab me and stick another gram of crystal into me. I was so busy cackling like a chicken that when I got up to get a pack of cigarettes, the hands on my watch moved three hours before I finally traveled the distance from the table to the door.

During this period, I was living at home and getting the money for speed by selling it, stealing, or burglarizing. I would lie out with my friends and show up at home whenever I needed a bath and a change of clothes. I came and went as I pleased.

I rubbed shoulders with people like the big-time speed dealer who was so crazy he would kill anyone for seven hundred dollars. He kept a gun strapped under each arm because he was absolutely paranoid about getting caught. His short haircut and vested suits made him look for all the world like someone straight.

We speed freaks understood one another's craziness. Once I came home and discovered Sam and another buddy running out of my parents' house. I didn't understand that they were stealing things. If I had, I would have helped them carry all the stuff out the door and received a cut of the speed they bought with the loot. I was that crazy!

One day Sam's father, who was a doctor, came into possession of five cases of pharmaceutical methamphetamine. Sam called me, his voice shaking in anticipation. "Get over here!" he said. When I saw what he had, I felt like a kid on Christmas morning. Sam began slowly but surely ripping off one bottle at a time and selling it. One day when I rang his doorbell and found him away, I got into the house through the back door, grabbed myself a bottle, and sold it for seventy-five dollars, with enough speed left over to keep me awake a few nights.

I didn't see anything wrong with stealing from my buddy. We both were stabbing each other in the back as hard as we could, but nothing really mattered to us. We just shrugged our shoulders as much as to say, "Well, you screwed me and I screwed you, and it's really okay. Because we understand craziness."

Once I burglarized the house of another friend to earn seventy-five dollars. I took a fine stereo, a TV and guns. When I gave the seventy-five dollars to Sam for some more speed, he spent the money himself. He told me he just forgot about the seventy-five dollars for which I had taken such a risk. I wasn't mad. Being on speed myself, I understood.

I began to tire of speed when I was twenty-two. One morning our gang was all "wired" when someone brought some heroin. Several people cooked it down and shot up. I collected all the cotton they left in their spoons, washed the heroin out of it, and did me a hit. Heroin just knocked me out. I thought I was in heaven. Immediately it took away all the pain I felt from being awake three days and nights on speed.

Yes, I fell in love with heroin. For awhile I just took

other people's cotton. Eventually I started buying my own heroin when I could scrape together twenty dollars from my intermittent jobs at a gas station. Most of the time I had only enough money to smoke pot, drink, and do downers.

I never thought that I would become a junkie. The first time I shot up heroin two days in a row, I expected to get a strung-out feeling on the third day. But I got no physical reaction at all. If I could do it for two or three days, why did I need to worry about ever getting addicted?

After I had used heroin on a daily basis for a couple of weeks, I found that I had developed a little bitty habit that was not really bad, just uncomfortable. I talked Dad into prescribing some downers for me so that I could withdraw and I did.

So, I didn't get addicted to heroin. The thing I did get hooked on was Dolophines—a prescription narcotic. For two dollars I could buy enough Dolophines to equal the effects of a paper of heroin—which cost forty dollars at the time.

Soon I was buying fifty Dolophines at a time and taking a handful a day. Even so, I was a real amateur compared to my buddy, Sam. He was doing twenty-eight a day!

By the time I was twenty-four, the Dolophine source dried up, but a government methadone program had begun in Houston. At first I bought other addicts' methadone. But then I told myself it was silly to pay fifteen dollars for the same amount that would cost me only seven dollars a week if I got myself enrolled in the methadone program. So I went down to the clinic wth my dirty urine specimens and signed on.

My life now revolved around drugs. Occasionally I worked as a mechanic, but usually I did nothing. My daily routine became to visit the methadone clinic every morning, go to my buddy Andy's home and sit around watching "The Three Stooges" and "The Flying Nun" on television. We smoked a little pot. Then I'd go home and sleep till about seven that evening, eat my one meal of the day, and hit the bars and drink. One good thing about methadone, I thought, was that I could down ten drinks and never feel a thing.

I remained in this same foggy routine for about nine to ten months. I kept on asking for more and more methadone until I finally was on ninety milligrams a day.

If anyone had asked me then what my future held, I probably would have said that someday I would go on Welfare and stay registered on the methadone program until I died at an early age, or I would kick some time and then get addicted again. These seemed to be the only alternatives open to me.

At last a friend of my mother's told her about a new organization named PDAP that worked with young drug addicts. Mom went to the counselor right away. Then she introduced the idea of going to PDAP to me.

Don't ask me what my mother or the counselor said to me. At the time I was on so much methadone that I couldn't feel a thing. I was practically anesthetized.

But the first meeting I attended was enough to wake up something in me. For the first time in years I felt something other than depression and a knot of pain in my stomach. It was almost like feeling a new baby jumping inside of me. With a spurt of joy, I felt that there was actually something left in me that was good. I wasn't all bad, all depressed! I fed on that feeling.

Since PDAP was so new, it had yet to work out a relationship with a hospital where I could go to detoxify. So I tried kicking on my own. Soon I won the nickname of "Methadone Bill."

I would sit at meetings giving every outward appearance of being totally depressed. My head would be down on my chest. But I was beginning to cut down on the methadone.

When it came my time to share during a meeting, I would say, "Hi, my name's Bill and I cut down another five milligrams on my methadone this week."

"Heyyy, all right!" was the general response. Everyone seemed real impressed. I kept cutting down and working on getting sober for two to three months.

But despite all my new-found optimism, I wasn't altogether sure I could kick completely. I had saved back some reserves of methadone. When my dose was cut down to zero, I took them. Now I saw I just wasn't going to make it! I returned to the methadone clinic. But when the doctor refused to give me more than five milligrams, I was so angry I dumped the methadone in his lap. He promptly escorted me to the door. Now I had done it. I had kissed the methadone program off completely!

What was I going to do? All I could think about was how sick I was going to be trying to kick cold turkey. I was really nervous. Here I had been around PDAP all this time and I still hadn't been able to kick. What the

----, I thought. I started shooting dope again. I left PDAP.

Then I got a surprise. Dad and Mom informed me I could no longer live at home. I wasn't real happy about that.

"You're really serious?" I asked. After all, I had been living at home for twenty-five years and my parents had never done anything except try to help me. It didn't make sense that when I was back into doping that they were going to kick me out of the house with no help at all.

At the time I didn't realize they were acting on the advice of the PDAP counselors. My mind was so foggy that two more years passed before I realized that the counselors and my parents were tricking me into getting sober. I knew that my parents were going to PDAP meetings and listening to the other parents. I saw that they were living differently, too. But at the time I didn't realize they were making changes in order to give me the chance to make my own decision to get sober.

So I went to stay with my friend, Andy. I started shooting a paper of heroin a day. But I knew my money was running out fast. I wasn't eating and I was getting real skinny. I began to fantasize about my nightmarish future. I saw myself as weak as a cat, unable to lift the television set which I was trying to steal out of someone's apartment. I couldn't hold a job or make any money. I was in a corner!

Now I decided I would try to kick with alcohol. But my old friend, booze, did nothing but make me sick. The only thing left was to drag myself down to PDAP and tell the counselor how scared I felt about kicking. I told him I just couldn't do it cold turkey.

He suggested that I go to an alternative program which was underwritten by the government. In this program I would be hospitalized to withdraw. He made me promise to live in the alternative house for six months before I returned to PDAP.

This time when I entered the hospital, I was scared to death. I wanted to get straight, but I couldn't stand the thought of the pain of kicking. Yet I knew that if I didn't go to a hospital, I would "one-last-time" myself to death with more dope.

When the doctor cut me back to nothing, I was so scared that I tried to sign myself out. But my parents put a restraining order on me so that I couldn't leave. I was thrown into a seclusion room to wake up the next morning on my first day of sobriety.

Well, kicking was bad, but not too bad. I didn't get very sick at my stomach. I had a lot of pain in my back and legs and I was nervous. But the biggest pain was between my ears. My thinking was all negative.

On the first night I didn't sleep at all. The next night I could only sleep about thirty minutes. The staff let me pace the floors whenever I wanted.

Throughout all that first week I held on to the idea that I was really going to get sober. I was going to make it this time. I had been to enough PDAP meetings that some of the things I had heard from others who had made it stuck with me. I kept thinking about the slogans, such as "Keep it simple," or "Put one foot in front of the other," or "Don't get into the thinking." Even away from PDAP I felt a lot of positive reinforcement from the group.

I kept reminding myself, too, about how PDAP-ers said most dope fiends wound up dead, in jail, or in mental hospitals. Well, I was already in this mental hospital, kicking. I knew that this was my best shot at getting sober and making it.

So I took hot baths, started eating, and began to gain weight. I did everything the staff told me to do to feel better. After three weeks I was discharged to the alternative house.

The philosophy about how to get straight in this program was completely opposite from PDAP's. Everything was so structured that their tough love was more "tough" than it was "love."

In this house, new residents started at the bottom, sweeping floors, raking leaves, and doing all the dirty work. Only when they progressed to the top of the seniority ladder could they tell everyone else what to do. No resident could curse or express feelings. In fact, residents had to learn how to take a lot of screaming and yelling from the staff because that was part of the conditioning that was thought to help them get straight.

But I knew how to handle getting screamed at. All my life I'd let others yell while I silently took it. So, when I found myself "getting a haircut"—that is, being disciplined by standing in a circle of five screaming, yelling ex-addicts—I didn't yell back.

Now that I have been in PDAP and realize how badly I needed to express feelings, I know that my silence was the worst reaction I could have had. I just held on to my bad feelings and got more depressed. It would have been better for me if I had flown back at them in a rage.

My mind was still so foggy that when the residents told me I couldn't make it in the outside straight world, I halfway believed them. But I argued.

"What do you mean I would never make it?" I would say. "There are plenty of ex-addicts in PDAP who are making it. They don't have to be locked up in this kind of place."

But when one of the residents retorted that I would go to jail for five years if I left the house, what he said seemed to make sense. Being on methadone fogs out your mind so badly that you can't really think. Before I went to the hospital, I had cut back to nine milligrams of methadone a day and I seriously wanted to get straight. So I was reading the Bible. I had quit eating meat. (I was so insane I thought my diet was making me unhealthy!) I thought that the comet, Kohoutek, was coming to push the world off its orbit, and that PDAP was God's way of giving me a last chance to get right before Judgment Day.

As crazy as all this sounds, I guess I am really glad for this twisted thinking because without it I might not have been motivated to get off drugs. I am also grateful for the alternative program, because without it I might not have been able to kick at all. At the alternative house I got a lot of tough, hard, "you-are-responsible" kind of stuff shoved down my throat. I really needed it to help me make it.

But I didn't like it. And I knew PDAP offered a better way of making it on the outside. So I split. I left the alternative house and went to my grandmother's.

Soon I received a phone call from a PDAP counselor. His voice radiated so much love I reacted almost in shock. I had experienced nothing but hostility in months. The counselor said he would let me back in PDAP even though I hadn't fulfilled my commitment of six months at the alternative house. Now I knew I was on the way to a new life.

For my first year in PDAP I lived at home and watched my parents change a lot. They could sleep at night for the first time in ages without having to worry if I was going to end up dead or in jail.

Mom told me that when I had been in such bad shape with drugs, she often prayed that I would die. She wanted my suffering to be over, both for my sake as well as for her own. She felt that there was nothing she and Dad could do to "fix me" despite the thousands of dollars they spent on hospitals.

Soon I got a construction job. After two and a half months, my employer moved to another town. He offered to pay me extra if I would commute. What a lot of positive strokes I got from that! The boss really liked me. For once in my life I was doing a good job. But I didn't want to commute, so I quit. For awhile I just recuperated at home, went to the PDAP day center, and got some more cobwebs out of my mind.

Eventually I enrolled in a trade school to learn drafting, but continued to go to PDAP's night meetings. I made the steering committee. As fist maker I gave a whole lot of people their monkey's fists and loved it.

A year after I entered PDAP, I was asked to go to work as a senior counselor. In those early days of PDAP, counselors didn't work up from junior to senior level. I didn't really want to drop the drafting classes before I finished, but I wanted approval so badly that I said yes to PDAP. Besides, I had a lot of the crusader in me. I felt I really wanted to show other addicts how to get straight.

Looking back, I can see that I was not really ready to be a counselor. When you first get sober, it takes about a year and a half before you become aware of what you are really feeling at the time you feel it. At times almost all ex-addicts get into something they call a "black hole," or a "blue funk" or a "bubble." I was no different. I would get into a bubble for a day at a time and feel depressed. Yet I would not really allow myself to feel what I was feeling. I would be confused.

The problem was that while everyone else in PDAP saw me as a successful counselor, I still *felt* like the failure I had always been. I still thought of myself as a loser. In the first PDAP center where I was a counselor, I told myself it was my fault that not enough people were coming in for appointments.

Then I was transferred to the PDAP staff at the hospital which had begun using PDAP counselors in its substance abuse program. In this position I would be able to do a lot of growing. Yet I saw the transfer as a put-down. I had been inadequate. No, I wasn't getting high as I used to, but I was wearing the face of a winner and feeling like a loser.

When I was asked to go to another city which was starting a new PDAP center, I agreed to go. I decided I would either make it or break it as a counselor there. Well, I broke it! I found a neat bunch of teen-agers and parents with whom to work, but I still had the wrong attitude. If there was a problem, I came down like a ton of bricks. I felt I had to control everything. When I saw I couldn't control anything, I tightened up even more.

Ex-addicts sometimes try to escape into sex, food, or other kinds of craziness in order to compensate for the loss of drugs. My compulsiveness took the form of assuming pressures that weren't really mine. Being a counselor automatically means you take on a hell of a lot of pressures. But I was taking on more than I had to.

I decided that I could perform in a job outside of PDAP with a tenth of the effort I was putting out as a counselor. Compared to most "normal" people I would still be a superman. After all, most folks out in the world were getting a little bit high all the time in order to function. With my sobriety, I could beat anything that any average person did on a job.

When I resigned from PDAP, I put my drafting skills to work with immediate success. I began making good money. I found a lot of satisfaction in my job. During my first year I also took thirteen hours in junior college engineering courses. My teacher told me he thought I was a highly skilled professional.

I credit the Twelve Steps with my success. When I joined PDAP they were a formula to get straight. Now I look on them as a way of practicing honesty, of giving up my will and letting God's will work in me, of helping other people.

To be honest not only means always double-checking my moncy to be sure I'm not shortchanging someone, but also being aware of my feelings. I have to realize what's really going on with me and not fool myself. Yes, sometimes reality hurts, but it sure beats the alternatives. The Twelve Steps have bought me an extra five years of life, because that's how long I've been sober.

I still go to PDAP meetings. I still feel that a good part of my life has to be spent in giving to other people. By staying sober, living an honest life, being responsible, getting to work on time, and paying my bills, I can be an example. I can serve a useful function within PDAP, even though I am not a counselor.

A lot of people try to say that ex-addicts like myself get so dependent on PDAP that they can't cope without the group. But I know how to make friends and be in a social gathering on the outside without having to get high. I have a new friend at work who used to smoke pot but now has had seven days of sobriety. I don't know if his sobriety is a result of my influence or example, but I have shared my experiences with him. I see miracles like that happening all around me.

My boss is a very spiritual man, very much into self-awareness. He has never smoked pot or gotten high or drunk. At least once a week we sit down and enjoy lunch together and have fantastic conversations. It is a real pleasure to be with him.

But I find it far more satisfying to remain a part of PDAP than to live without it. I share an apartment with another PDAP-er who is a counselor. I go to meetings, I sponsor people. I tell my experiences. When new people come into PDAP, I often put them up in my apartment. Many people in this city who are now sober say I helped them get started over a year ago.

That's a good feeling. It is as if PDAP has given me something to live for, now that it's saved my life.

The Twelve Steps of PDAP

1. We admitted that mind-changing chemicals had caused at least part of our lives to become unmanageable.
2. We found it necessary to *"Stick with Winners"* in order to grow.
3. We realized that a Higher Power, expressed through our love for each other, can help restore us to sanity.
4. We made a decision to turn our will and our lives over to the care of God, as we understand Him.
5. We made a searching and fearless moral inventory of ourselves.
6. We admitted to God, to ourselves, and to another human being the exact nature of our wrongs.
7. We became willing to allow our Higher Power, through the love of the group, to help change our way of life and humbly asked Him to help us change.
8. We made a list of all persons we had harmed and became willing to make amends to them all.
9. We made direct amends to such people, whenever possible, except when to do so would injure them, others, or ourselves.
10. We have continued to look at ourselves and when wrong, promptly admitted it.
11. We have sought through prayer and meditation to improve our conscious contact with our Higher Power, that we have chosen to call God, praying only for knowledge of His will for us and courage to carry that out.
12. We, having had a Spiritual awakening as a result of these steps, tried to carry our love and understanding to others, and to practice these principles in our daily lives.

Chapter Ten

The Twelve
Steps

As you read the preceding chapters, you may have felt that PDAP-ers, young and old, hold an exaggerated reverence for the Twelve Steps of PDAP. You may look at the Steps as they are reproduced on page 130 and think that nothing so simple could change lives!

But it is not the reading of the Twelve Steps that has revitalized the people whose stories you have read. It has been the living of them.

When PDAP-ers talk about working the program, they mean that they are making the choice of applying the Steps in a moment-by-moment response to the events in their lives. They are choosing to change resentments into unconditional love, self-pity into self-esteem, and fears into self-knowledge that can be dealt with firmly and positively.

At parent meetings you might hear the following paragraphs read:

"Having lived with the problems caused by drugs, most of us are emotionally upset as a result of strain, stress, distorted thinking, fears, resentments, self-pity, and other negative factors.

"We have had to turn from an attitude of defeat and frustration to a new way of life where positive thinking is the keynote. . . .

"The Twelve Steps of PDAP which we try to follow are not easy! At first we may think that some of them are unnecessary. But if we are honest with ourselves, we will find that they all apply to us as well as to the drug abuser. The benefit derived from a strict and constant observance of them can be limitless."

Many have found that it was when the future seemed the darkest that they were willing to choose to work the Twelve Steps. They then carried out their decision by going to Step Studies and topic meetings. They listened to the ways other parents have found to apply the Steps to their lives. Because others allowed themselves to become vulnerable enough to the group to admit their own character defects, they were able to identify some truths about themselves. Yet they were not discouraged. They saw that if others could change, they could, too.

Talking about the Steps with others is the most effective way of learning to apply them to one's own life. However, this chapter includes some of the points that are frequently brought out in Step Studies by parents of drug abusers. There is no one official PDAP interpretation of the Twelve Steps. They say as many different things as there are people. Bear in mind that these are the Twelve Steps as one person sees them.

It may be that as you read this chapter, you will see that your purpose in reading this book is far different from the one with which you started. It may be that you will choose to step out of the observer role and into an active one. If so, your rewards will be many, for the Steps are the basis for spiritual growth. As parents find a new relationship to their Higher Power, the problems which brought them to PDAP are corrected. They also find themselves living peacefully, contentedly, and joyfully in a way they never believed possible for themselves.

Here, then, are the Twelve Steps:

STEP ONE: WE ADMITTED THAT MIND-CHANGING CHEMICALS HAD CAUSED AT LEAST PART OF OUR LIVES TO BECOME UNMANAGE-ABLE.

Which of us wants to admit that a part of our lives has become unmanageable because of mind-changing chemicals? Yet, which of us has not felt so depressed, terrified, or angry that we have been practically immobilized as we watched the steady decline of our youngsters?

"We have not invited anyone to our house in over a year, because we feared that others would see what was happening," reported a mother.

"I am so angry at my son for doping that I wish he would die. I just want him out of my life," a father admitted with shame.

"I could not concentrate on my work because I kept

133

expecting a phone call that would tell me our daughter was dead or in jail," said still another.

Our lives have become unmanageable in other ways, too. Some of us have tried so hard to control our children, to "make" them stop doping, that we have beaten them. We have locked them in rooms. We have found ourselves screaming and yelling. Others of us have tried to drown our feelings of failure in alcohol, or given in to continuous depression.

While most of us can relate to at least some of that behavior, few of us really want to admit that our lives are unmanageable. We are adults, aren't we? Many of us have status in the community, responsible jobs, positions in clubs and organizations that give us the impression that we are very much in control of our lives. Who wants to admit powerlessness? The very thought of it seems defeating. Yet this Step tells us that accepting our powerlessness to control our feelings, to influence our children, to change all the "others" in our lives is the very first Step to a new way of life. We accept the fact that we are the only persons we can do anything about and free ourselves from the guilt many of us feel for having a drug abuser or for having been a less-than-perfect parent.

We no longer have to try to "make" our children stop doping. We can go on to practice "tough love." We can with a free conscience stop "padding their corners" with room, board, and money that will make it easy for them to continue to dope. We know that all the corner-padding in the world will only make it easier for them to avoid taking responsibility for their own lives.

Once we experience the freedom to be found in

simply admitting that our lives are unmanageable and we ourselves are powerless over others, we will be overjoyed to practice Step One in our lives.

STEP TWO: WE FOUND IT NECESSARY TO *STICK WITH WINNERS* IN ORDER TO GROW.

Of course our teen-agers must avoid being with their old doping buddies. They must stick with winners— PDAP-ers who are sober and motivated to practice love and understanding.

But who are the winners and losers in our own lives? Our wonderful PDAP friends are winners because they are willing to love us and stand by us. Our PDAP sponsors listen to us, share feelings with us, and challenge us to grow.

Who are the losers in our lives? Many of us have had to recognize that in the past we gravitated to those friends or relatives who played psychological games with us. In their presence, we have allowed ourselves to feel guilty or inferior. Because of our low self-esteem, we have been all too willing to cling to the blame and punishment they dole out.

Probably these "losers" are not losers for everyone. They may be motivated to wreak psychological damage on us more because of their own internal problems rather than because of anything we have done. But the fact remains that for us they are losers. We do not need to take on anyone else's problems and make them our own.

It is simple to avoid seeing or being with losers to whom we have no close relationship. When the losers in our lives are within our families, the solution is harder. Many of us have learned to give these people the choice of changing their "losing" behavior or accepting the fact that we can no longer be with them.

As we have learned to practice Step Two, we have become better able to love ourselves—and hence to love others—for doing so.

STEP THREE: WE REALIZED THAT A HIGHER POWER, EXPRESSED THROUGH OUR LOVE FOR EACH OTHER, CAN HELP RESTORE US TO SANITY.

For many of us, Step Three can be a stumbling block for two reasons. First, some of us may never have had any conception of a Higher Power, or we may have had the wrong conception of a Higher Power. Second, we do not like the implication that we have done something crazy enough to need to be restored to sanity.

But many of us who were agnostics have successfully worked the Twelve Steps. We found that when we could not accept the idea of a Higher Power, we could recognize the love that PDAP parents had for us and for one another. For, when we felt that we could not face another day like the one we had just been through with our drug abuser, we could go to a PDAP parent meeting and receive enough strength to keep going. It was then simple to accept the fact that the group was actually a Higher Power than ourselves.

Many of us rejected the idea of a Higher Power because we were taught that God was keeping score of our wrongs to punish us. But those farther along in PDAP told us that their Higher Power was one who loves, trusts, and forgives us when we are not perfect. As we saw this same kind of loving behavior being practiced in the group, we were able to believe.

Once we had found our Higher Power, we then had to become aware of the particular forms of insanity we had been practicing. We did not use this information to browbeat ourselves, but to identify it and allow our Higher Power to overcome it.

Did we at one time believe that we could protect our children against life's hard knocks by making excuses for their misbehavior? By refusing to allow them to make a mistake? Did we believe that we were responsible for their unhappiness? These were forms of insanity which masqueraded under the name of "parental love."

Did we believe that by forcing our children to follow our own rules about going to school, doing homework, and getting out of bed in the mornings we could "teach" them self-discipline? That attitude was an insanity, for self-discipline comes to each person on his or her own efforts.

Did we take on the responsibility for our spouse's happiness or unhappiness? Did we punish ourselves by believing we did not deserve to have time to ourselves to enjoy? Did we always say yes to every request made to us, because we felt we "ought" to do what others, rather than we, wished to do? Did we always go along with what everyone else said was right instead of following our own inner convictions? These responses, too, were forms of insanity.

Step Three says that there is a Higher Power which can restore us to sanity. Originally we may not have believed that we needed restoration. But there are few of us PDAP parents who after working the program for a few months cannot look back and shake our heads in amazement at the many insane things we once did.

STEP FOUR: WE MADE A DECISION TO TURN OUR WILL AND OUR LIVES OVER TO THE CARE OF GOD, AS WE UNDERSTAND HIM.

Now comes another Step that many find hard. Step Four says that we are to turn our will and our lives over to this Higher Power that we may barely recognize. How can we do it?

For most of us, the ability to "let go and let God" came one step at a time. We started by trying to release our children, to put them in his care rather than in our own. Many of us had to give our teen-agers the difficult choice of getting straight or moving from our homes. Or, after we thought they were straight, we had to watch them slip while we did nothing to help them find their way back to PDAP.

The emotional pain we felt in our powerlessness to prevent our children from suffering was motivation enough to find a Higher Power to whom we could turn over our will and our lives. Willingness in this area of our existence came easily.

From these small beginnings, we saw that our Higher Power did work far better than we ever could. We then went on to turn our will and our lives over to him in other matters besides our children. When we learned to pray, "Thy will, not mine, be done," many of us were surprised to find that we did not sink into a state of unhealthy dependence on Another. Instead, we found ourselves living with more freedom, happiness, and power than we had ever had before.

But this Step is a tricky one. Some of us have confused willingness with self-will. We have felt that if we just tried hard enough to turn our lives and wills over to God, then we could "fix" our drug abusers and make ourselves perfect. We have had to learn that such an attitude is just another way of trying to see that *our* will, not God's, is done.

Yes, we must make a concerted effort to *want* to be willing to turn our lives over to God. But we recognize that we cannot make anything happen that we want to happen. We must wholeheartedly do our footwork— practice PDAP's principles, prayers, and slogans, while letting God change our lives as he wills. The timing is his, not ours. Once we give up trying so hard, we often find that all is accomplished, how we do not know.

So, the decision to be willing is the key to working Step Four. Our Higher Power will enable us to transcend our human limitations.

STEP FIVE: WE MADE A SEARCHING AND FEARLESS MORAL INVENTORY OF OURSELVES.

Many of us have felt a great reluctance to work Step Five. We have not thought it necessary to look deeply at our strengths and weaknesses. We have felt there was nothing wrong with us that seeing our drug abusers get straight would not make all right. Others of us have been so filled with guilt that we have been afraid to spend time looking at feelings of which we were ashamed. We spent all our efforts trying desperately to hide our moral failures.

But since we learned in the earlier Steps to trust our Higher Power, we recognize in this Step that we need not dread punishment for our weaknesses. We can see that by admitting those defects we want to change, we will receive nothing but love and forgiveness.

When other parents give glowing reports on how they have "gotten rid of the garbage" in their lives by doing an inventory, we realize they are able to concentrate on their strengths rather than their weaknesses. We then feel encouraged to look at our own character defects.

We have written our inventories in many different ways. Some of us have followed a questionnaire supplied by the group which enabled us to look at our feelings, fears, and resentments from infancy.

Others of us have taken the traditional list of the "seven deadly sins"—pride, greed, lust, anger, gluttony, envy, and laziness—with which to compare our lives. Still others have used one page for writing down the things we liked about our lives, and another page for the things that have been painful.

No matter how we do the inventory, we have all learned that being completely thorough is the key to making this Step work for us. We have found it necessary to think deeply to avoid blaming others for the painful events in our lives. We have had to force ourselves to put down on paper the things of which we were ashamed.

We have had to trace the origins of our feelings of resentment and self-pity, our guilt, or our sexual problems. And often we have found that the basis for all of them has been fear.

By doing our inventories, we gain a great deal of self-knowledge that was previously hidden from us. We have inevitably found that we have harmed many persons because of our emotions. We cannot grow in our spiritual development without this self-revelation. Yet we have nothing to fear from it. Indeed, the inventory is a way to find a new freedom and self-love that will forever stand us in good stead.

STEP SIX: WE ADMITTED TO GOD, TO OUR-SELVES AND TO ANOTHER HUMAN BEING THE EXACT NATURE OF OUR WRONGS.

Sharing our character defects with a Higher Power whom we trust may be relatively easy for many of us, but admitting them to another person seems at first impossible. Why do we who have already completed this Step feel that such sharing is necessary?

"Because there is a great release in doing it," one PDAP parent may say.

"Because only by sharing my inventory with another did I learn to accept myself as a child of God, different and unique, but basically like other members of the human race. It brought me humility," said another.

Others report that after sharing their inventories, they were more able to share themselves with other people. They could allow themselves to become vulnerable enough to admit their mistakes, to take the blame for things they had done wrong. They learned to admit to their teen-agers that they, too, made mistakes. They found a new level of intimacy with their mates.

By finding the right person with whom we could share an inventory, we benefited a great deal. Such a person was sponsor, friend, clergyman, therapist, or someone who was nonjudgmental and could gently help us overcome the self-justification we were prone to feel while trying to admit our wrongs. Such persons also helped us see the positive things about ourselves.

STEP SEVEN: WE BECAME WILLING TO ALLOW OUR HIGHER POWER, THROUGH THE LOVE OF THE GROUP, TO HELP CHANGE OUR WAY OF LIFE AND HUMBLY ASKED HIM TO HELP US CHANGE.
Now the willingness and self-knowledge we had attained in the previous Steps enabled us to work Step Seven. We learned we could do more than just turn our lives and our wills over to his care. We recognized that we actually did have character defects which we had been unaware of, and that we had harmed others unintentionally. We asked him to help us change, and we trusted him to do the work while we faithfully practiced PDAP's principles.

Many of us found that God truly did change us. How or exactly when he accomplished it, we do not know. We just found ourselves giving up our old self-justifications, our blaming other people, our refusal to be kind to ourselves.

We recognized that the love of the group played its part. We went to meetings and listened to others share their feelings, fears, and strengths. Then we were able to select the actions that we felt might work in our own lives and try them out. We allowed our sponsors to challenge us to grow. In our willingness to make choices and to allow God to free us for a different way of life, we changed in a slow and gradual way.

STEP EIGHT: WE MADE A LIST OF ALL PERSONS WE HAD HARMED AND BECAME WILLING TO MAKE AMENDS TO THEM ALL.
While making our inventories, many of us also made a list of people we had harmed and the ways we had done so. If not, we now sat down and did so.

It was only as we were able to use the new-found

humility we learned in Step Seven that we were able to admit truly, without self-justification, without trying to protect ourselves, that we did indeed harm many other people, including relatives, friends, and enemies. Now we had to become willing to make amends to them all—even to those who, because they had hurt us, we considered our enemies.

Once again willingness became the key to heightening our spiritual development. We had to recognize that we were carrying a big load of guilt because of what we had consciously or unconsciously done to others. We found it much easier to rationalize and make excuses for our past conduct than to face others and admit our wrongs. For ourselves as well as for others, we had to get rid of resentments and grudges. If we did not, we knew they would destroy our serenity.

When we became willing to make amends to others, we were able to rise above the need to blame others, to hate, to criticize. In doing so, we learned to love and respect others, even when they were different from us, even when they could not be changed by us. We could, in so doing, learn to love ourselves.

STEP NINE: WE MADE DIRECT AMENDS TO SUCH PEOPLE, WHENEVER POSSIBLE, EXCEPT WHEN TO DO SO WOULD INJURE THEM, OTHERS OR OURSELVES.

Once we had the willingness to make amends to all those whom we had harmed, the next step was to go to the persons involved, tell them (or write to them if they were elsewhere) about the things we did wrong, and ask their forgiveness. If what we had done required financial restitution as well, we were willing to make it.

If we were afraid to make amends to those we had harmed, we had only to remember the humility learned in the previous Steps. We knew if we asked humbly that our Higher Power give us courage, he would do so.

If still we were not ready, we could wait until we had developed the faith to do so, resting in the assurance that our Higher Power would surely give it to us if we continued to ask for it.

In making amends, we needed to think of the other persons as well as ourselves. If our words would harm them, we could make our amends simply by changing as much as possible our behavior to them.

For instance, some had doping teen-agers who were still at the point where they blamed their parents for their drug abuse and all the resulting misfortunes in their lives. These parents could not help their youngsters by telling them how they felt about harming them in the past. They found it far better to make their amends by continuing to love them and by constantly turning them over to God. Once the teen-agers had worked their own programs sufficiently to receive the amends vocally, the parents could make them.

On the other hand, we found we had to be careful not to justify ourselves and refuse to make amends to others simply because they were not ready to forgive us. We reminded ourselves that asking forgiveness of such people is necessary if we are to overcome our own guilt and low self-esteem. In making such amends we could rise above the need to blame others, to hate, to criticize. And in doing so we could be freed to love all the world, including ourselves. We did not have to take on the other person's refusal to forgive, since we could practice

Step One's powerlessness over others. We could accept them as they were.

STEP TEN: WE HAVE CONTINUED TO LOOK AT OURSELVES AND WHEN WRONG, PROMPTLY ADMITTED IT.

Now that we have worked through the "house-cleaning" of the first nine Steps, we are ready for the "maintenance Steps"—those which enable us to continue to enjoy our lives and to grow in the future.

Our spiritual development can never be complete. We can never relax and feel, "I've got it made." Yet for many of us, the growth that we see in ourselves as we use the maintenance Steps becomes the most exciting part of our lives. We joyfully work the last three Steps on a daily basis. We find ourselves happier, more fulfilled, more excited to be alive and in the world than ever before. The last three Steps are the nutritious diet which strengthens us.

In Step Ten we find it necessary to work three kinds of inventories. First we use a "spot check" inventory—a frequent short review of our actions, thoughts, and motives—several times a day. The spot check inventory allows us to be aware of our wrongs at the time they happen. With such knowledge we are able to admit promptly what we have done and make immediate amends. We never have to carry a load of guilt very long.

A second type of inventory is the review, made shortly before going to bed. We look honestly and objectively at all the activities of the day. We admit our wrongs, but do not try to condemn ourselves. Instead we consider ways to make amends in the future, the very next day if possible. Sleep comes quickly when we let go of our imperfections in this way.

A third type of inventory is the long-term periodic one, done whenever the need is felt. It may be almost as detailed as the Step Five inventory. Its object is to give us a perspective of the way we have changed.

In this inventory, we find that many of the problems and character defects from which we suffered in the past have truly vanished. We also may find that there are others of which we were not previously aware. These will require spiritual attention now.

By using all three kinds of inventories, we can assure ourselves that we will continue to be honest with ourselves. We will keep on growing.

STEP ELEVEN: WE HAVE SOUGHT THROUGH PRAYER AND MEDITATION TO IMPROVE OUR CONSCIOUS CONTACT WITH OUR HIGHER POWER, THAT WE HAVE CHOSEN TO CALL GOD, PRAYING ONLY FOR KNOWLEDGE OF HIS WILL FOR US AND COURAGE TO CARRY THAT OUT.

In this joyful maintenance Step, we seek to improve our contact with God. Some of us had to learn how to pray and to meditate, for we had never learned it in the past. We had thought that those things "just weren't for us." Or we had been sure that we could control our lives without them. Perhaps we had been bitter that God did not run the world the way we thought he should. For whatever reason, we had to admit that we were completely ignorant of the way to go about staying in contact with God.

Most parents of drug abusers, however, had probably made some attempts to pray long before trying to work this Step. Many of us had asked God to make our children stop doping and had petitioned God to take care of sons or daughters who were driven to do the many dangerous things that drug abusers do. It is likely that if we had been telling God what to do in this way and had not seen any results, we felt there was little value to prayer. We had to learn to pray that God's will—not ours—be done in our lives and in our children's lives, before we could truly pray. The earlier Steps were a preparation for this one.

As we became willing to let God work his changes in our lives and our children's lives, we learned that we could come quietly to him. We could lift our hearts to him and make our petitions. The peace and security that we received convinced us of the value of prayer.

We may have thought that meditation was something of a fad. We learned, however, that it is a simple process of focusing one's attention on the Higher Power rather than on oneself or on the conscious activities of the day.

One PDAP parent meditates simply by stilling her mind, focusing it on the Higher Power, and waiting. "In prayer, I am reaching up to God, but in meditation I do not have to do anything other than to relax, still my mind, and let God come to me," she said. "During meditation my Higher Power often supplies me with answers to questions I have not even asked, but need. The answers may come during meditation or even at other times during the day."

The second part of this Step, "praying only for knowledge of His Will for us," was also learned in the earlier Steps. We continue to do our footwork. We go to meetings, we work our programs, we meditate and pray, we practice acceptance. But we do not try to tell God how to solve our problems. Our Higher Power knows what is best for us and our loved ones. We help him create his miracles when we put ourselves into his hands and become willing to do what he wants done.

It is important to ask God for the courage to carry out his will. Many times we do hear God asking us to "change the things we can"—ourselves. We may recognize that we need to learn to remain silent or to speak out; to hold our temper or to allow ourselves to feel and express anger. If we feel incapable of such change, we only have to ask for the courage and God will send us energy, backbone, and a power higher than our own to see us through.

STEP TWELVE: WE, HAVING HAD A SPIRITUAL AWAKENING AS A RESULT OF THESE STEPS, TRIED TO CARRY OUR LOVE AND UNDER-STANDING TO OTHERS, AND TO PRACTICE THESE PRINCIPLES IN OUR DAILY LIVES.

For many of us, practicing the Steps has brought about an instantaneous spiritual awakening. For others, the process has been more gradual, so that one day they simply realized that they had become different persons. In either case, a spiritual awakening brought a new relationship to God. We learned to experience him in every detail of our lives and recognized that it was a joy to give up our will to God and let him take over.

Once we have experienced such wonders, we will want to carry our love and understanding to others. But we quickly learn that the best way to do this is not only to tell people we love them, but also to express our love in actions.

At meetings we can share our experiences, the good and the bad. We can allow ourselves to become truly vulnerable to others. We can be sponsors. We can lead a meeting. We can have a "one-on-one" with someone. We can reveal our own strengths and weaknesses with which others can identify. We can accept others as they are, without trying to change them.

As we practice Step Twelve, we may be surprised to learn that we benefit even more than the persons we are trying to help. We find that it is true that "in giving we receive." By carrying our love and understanding to others without expecting any return, we are able to overcome our own depressions, angers, and fears. Reaching out to others, we learn to accept, love, and, be kind to ourselves.

Many of us, having made the choice to practice the Twelve Steps, have learned there is no more beautiful way to live.

Chapter Eleven

When Hospitalization Is Necessary

"Your teen-ager needs to go to the hospital."

Parents who have a son or daughter with a serious drug problem that has caused them to fear overdoses or criminal behavior may experience instant relief to these words. They may feel hopeful for the first time in years when the counselor tells them that a good hospital which specializes in treating chemical dependencies has a recovery rate of 80 percent.

But parents with youngsters who seem to have progressed in PDAP may argue, "It's true he has his slips. And I agree he seems to keep on seeing himself as a loser. But he's better than he was." They may panic, or even disbelieve that their youngster needs to be in a "mental hospital."

A counselor can assure these parents that thirty to ninety days spent in a good hospital can equal several years on the outside in PDAP. Teen-agers who are not quite making it in PDAP become motivated to get straight more quickly with the hospital's concentrated therapy.

Is there truly such a thing as a "good" hospital—one with a staff which understands drug abusers and knows how to work with them? PDAP has found some fine private institutions which have incorporated the PDAP program within their own treatment plan for drug abuse.

These hospitals are designed to provide inpatient or outpatient therapeutic services to individuals afflicted with alcohol dependency or problems; other chemical dependencies or problems; and related emotional disorders, such as stress, anxiety, tension, and depression.

A psychiatrist supervises the plan of treatment for each patient. A primary therapist is assigned to each patient for daily psychotherapy. In addition, patients attend daily group therapy meetings. They may learn relaxation methods through the use of biofeedback and neurotone. They become physically fit through a planned program of diversional therapy.

Former PDAP counselors, employed by the hospital and still active in PDAP, are valuable members of the team of professionals and paraprofessionals who work with patients. Their job is to help keep teens straight and provide valuable insights about the patients to the hospital staff. They hold daily PDAP topic meetings and do Twelve-Step counseling.

Advanced PDAP-ers are also employed as technical aides. Not only do they take temperatures, keep records, and talk to patients; they also function as a positive peer group.

In fact many of the hospital's workers—from cooks to biofeedback technicians—are PDAP-ers. In such a positive, loving atmosphere, patients are motivated to open up and level with a therapist.

These hospitals do not treat chemical addiction with further medication. They make use of few drugs, other than those prescribed for manic depressives whose chemical imbalance requires lifelong correction. Even patients who are addicted to heroin can be detoxified by using a benign, nonaddictive drug for about three days or less. Patients who are acting out and having serious problems may be prescribed an antipsychotic for a week or so until they can deal with their anxieties through therapy. Then their medication is eliminated.

Other than in the above cases, all patients function completely without any kind of drugs. The hospitals' PDAP-trained employees, charged with the discipline of the patients, make a strong effort to keep any kind of chemicals from being smuggled into the hospital.

When teen-agers enter these hospitals, they learn from counselors that they must obey three basic rules:
1. No coming to meetings high or holding (getting high while at a meeting).
2. No sex or sexual acting out.
3. No violence.

Teen-agers are warned that if they break any of these rules while hospitalized, they will receive "consequences"—one to three days of seclusion in their rooms. However, counselors and therapists use these solitary periods not as punishment, but as an opportunity to spend intensified time with patients at a moment when they are especially vulnerable to receiving help. They may ask patients to read relevant books or write out reasons why they did what they did. They may ask patients to make a long list of all the positive things they have ever done and all their likable qualities. For nine out of ten patients, seclusion turns out to be a very good experience.

Building self-esteem is one of the primary goals of the hospital treatment. Many patients who have always seen themselves as losers at first feel there is nothing about them that anyone could like. The therapists and PDAP-trained employees provide a warm and caring atmosphere in which these patients can learn to love themselves.

What can parents do to help their youngsters while they are in the hospital? The rather surprising advice is "work on yourselves."

Says a hospital counselor, "When patients are brought in, we ask the parents to let go of their teens. Most have been so tied up in their son's or daughter's troubles that they are pretty grim. We ask parents to learn to enjoy themselves once again, to renew their romantic interests. We may suggest that they let us care for their youngster while they go on a trip together."

During an orientation period, parents are asked to attend the regular PDAP parent meetings.

"Parents go through unbelievable pain when they have a drug abuser. They need a lot of nurturing, too. The most important thing for parents to do is to let go of their guilt. They should realize that peer pressure for their youngster to get into drugs has been very strong.

They don't need to punish themselves for their teen's involvement," said a counselor.

During the first five working days, parents are not allowed to visit their teen-agers in the hospital. When visits are allowed, counselors encourage parents to be positive with their youngsters.

A hospital spokesman who is not a PDAP member gives similar advice to parents who want to help.

"We ask parents to be supportive, but to realize that this is a time for their adolescents to do some things for themselves. We encourage parents to let us care for their youngster while they take care of themselves. There are usually other family members, too, who have not been able to get the attention they want because so much has been focused on the drug abuser.

"We tell parents to be themselves when they visit. If they have any questions they want to ask their adolescents, they should ask them. We don't keep any secrets from patients. If parents want to know something, they will be told in the presence of the adolescent. We encourage openness," said the staff member.

"If parents want to know what kind of drugs their youngsters have been taking, they should ask them. If the youngsters want to tell, they will. If not, parents should know that it's really not important to know."

Staff members point out that teen-agers who have been drug abusers are classic manipulators. When patients attempt to blame either the parents or other authority figures for their problems, it is important not to get "hooked" into taking the responsibility.

"We have a very nurturing program. We are a close

staff. We tell each other and the patients that we love each other. So the teen-agers have all the opportunities in the world to make some changes, but it is up to them as to how motivated they are to make the changes they need to make," said the hospital spokesman.

"The doors that lead to the drug treatment wing are locked to keep out mind-changing chemicals. But these doors are not locked from the inside. Patients may leave the hospital at any time they wish. But teen-agers also know that their parents may choose to place them somewhere they would like less if they do leave. They soon learn to make the decision to stay and work the program."

Counselors place patients in three groups, depending on their progress. In Group Three are the resistant patients and those who are still figuring out what is going on. When teen-agers make a decision to stay in the hospital for thirty days and show some action that proves they are serious about working the program, they are moved to Group Two. Then when patients start reaching out to others and becoming leaders, they are placed in Group One. Patients in Group One may spend half the day at the hospital and the other half at a PDAP center as they begin the transition to the outside world.

Patients who have reached the Group-Two level are allowed passes to go to PDAP meetings on the outside. They may attend PDAP parties or spend the weekend with their parents or with stable PDAP members.

When recovering youngsters who are free of chemicals and able to express love openly go to visit their homes, their parents may believe them "cured."

"I knew the problem was doping, and that if he could

just get straightened out, everything would be okay," is a comment often made by happy parents. But this reaction can lead to a trap.

A counselor says, "Parents see such a difference in their teen-agers that they don't realize all the intense work the youngsters have been putting in. While in the hospital they are scrutinized and watched all the time. Their behavior is being modified twenty-four hours a day.

"Parents don't see the bad times when a counselor tells the youngster his attitude stinks and the teen-ager runs to his room screaming, crying, and yelling. They don't know how long the tantrum lasts before he comes out and gruffly says, 'Okay, what do I need to do to change?'

"While teen-agers are at the hospital, the peer groups reinforce their desire to change. They need a positive peer group atmosphere at home, too."

These hospitals make no guarantees that ex-patients will continue to be straight, honest about themselves, and loving. But they do stress that parents who are working their own Twelve-Step programs will be better able to provide the positive atmosphere which their youngsters need if they are going to function on the outside.

When a youngster leaves the hospital, parents are encouraged to make an appointment with the counselor and decide on a program of action at home.

"Parents and teen-agers should make it clear to each other exactly what they expect of each other even before the youngster leaves the hospital. Each family can make its own rules, based on what the members want from each other. The important thing is for everyone to be clear about what is expected within the family relationship," said a counselor.

Sometimes counselors and therapists make the decision that it would be better for teen-agers not to return to their parents' home after leaving the hospital.

"Parents should realize that placements outside the family are a protection for both the parents and the teen-agers. Over the years a lot of psychological games have been set up. The hospital stay may not be long enough to break those patterns for either the teen-ager or the parents," a counselor said.

"Many youngsters do better living with a new family whom they want to impress. They will work hard to get the approval of these parent substitutes. After a couple of months or so, they learn to like their new behavior. Then they may be returned to their parents."

Parents can also lessen the pain by remaining active in their own PDAP parent groups. They can learn to enjoy themselves as individuals worthy in themselves apart from their role as parents. Many fathers and mothers have experienced joy and fulfillment through the revelation that when you love someone, you can let him go. For by doing so, you will find him coming back to you.

Parents should avoid having unrealistic expectations about their youngsters' behavior after leaving the hospital.

"Before Johnny is admitted to the hospital, he uses terrible language," said a staff member. "He's stoned all the time. He doesn't keep his room straight. A lot of parents expect that when he goes home, he's going to be neat and clean, ambitious, and motivated. He's not going to use the terrible language. He's not even going to smoke cigarettes.

"But Johnny will still be basically the same person he was before. The actual changes will be subtle. Parents can expect their discharged youngsters at least to be trying to make changes in their lives and to adhere to society's rules and regulations. They can be assured that their youngsters have been given some tools with which to work.

"We hope that when patients go home, parents can expect them to be drug-free youngsters who are going to school or to work, who are continuing to be involved in PDAP on a very active basis, and who are going to be able to take some responsibility for their behavior."

"One day at a time" is a slogan that has meaning to many parents who have welcomed a youngster home from the hospital, for they need much patience and acceptance. But parents can have realistic hopes if they practice gratitude for the advances already made and if they continue to depend on a Higher Power to make further changes.

They can be optimistic that they and their teen-agers will find a new and joyful way of living that they might never have known if they had not made the choice to work their own programs wholeheartedly.

The Future_____

Now that you have become acquainted with many parents of drug abusers, you will see that we are many different types.

We are angry. We are guilty. We are resentful. We are filled with self-pity.

Or, we are indignant. We are disgusted. We are terrified. We are bitter.

Yet, we are loving. We are kind. We are joyful. We are fulfilled.

We are all these things, the negative and the positive. The things we wish we weren't and the things we like about ourselves.

Our children are just as unique. They are angry. They are serene. They are hurting. They are loving. They are seeking an escape. They are searching for a solution.

We know that we can never change them. They have

their own choices to make, their own lives to live. We know that we can best help them by helping ourselves.

Perhaps the greatest gift that has been given to many of us parents in PDAP is to see ourselves as we are.

We see ourselves in the words and actions of other parents.

We see ourselves attempting to follow the Twelve Steps.

We see ourselves repeating the same self-defeating actions over and over, like some animated toy in a store window.

We see ourselves making choices to change. We love ourselves when the best we can do is pray, "God grant me the serenity to accept the things I cannot change, the courage to change the things I can, and the wisdom to know the difference."

We love ourselves when we struggle and fail and try again and grow.

We know that we will never be perfect, for our Higher Power will continue to reveal new truths about ourselves throughout our lifetime.

Yet we can be peaceful. We can be content. We can be full of joy. For we have found a way to see ourselves and our children as we are, and to love ourselves and our children no matter what we are like.

In PDAP we have found hope.